英文

日本 絵 とき事典 2

ILLUSTRATED
LIVING JAPANESE STYLE

[生活編]

ILLUSTRATED
LIVING JAPANESE STYLE

1st edition······Nov.,1984
15th edition······ Jan.,1997

Printed in Japan

About This Book

1) Layout

The book is in four parts: Living in Japan,
Enjoying Japan, Understanding Japan, and
Appendix: Japanese Self-Expression. Each part
contains a number of short illustrated articles
which can be read in any order; either for enjoy-
ment, or, using the index at the back of the
book, for reference.

2) Japanese Words

All the Japanese words in this book have been
romanized according to the Hepburn System.
They are printed in italics except when they
appear in headings or bold type. Long vowels are
indicated by a line above them, as in *'Shintō'*;
and accented e's at the ends of words are indicated by an acute accent, as in *'saké'* (pronounc-
ed "sa-keh").

Dear Readers,

When you visit Japan for the first time, don't expect to see the streets full of 'samurai' and 'geisha'. The lifestyle of the average Japanese has today become almost completely westernized. But beneath Japan's fast-moving, ultra-modern exterior, its unique culture and customs, shaped by centuries of tradition, live on.

This book is designed to help both residents and visitors to overcome cultural bafflement and get to know the "real Japan". Through pictures and explanations, it introduces many interesting aspects of modern Japanese life, and gives advice on how to behave in a variety of social situations.

We hope that readers will find this volume, along with its sister volume 'A LOOK INTO JAPAN', an easily-read and insightful guide into "LIVING JAPANESE STYLE".

CONTENTS

Living in Japan .... 住む

Enjoying Japan .... 遊ぶ

Understanding Japan ·· 学ぶ

Appendix .... 付録

FEATURE

LIVING

EXCHANGING GREETINGS

The Japanese bow (*'ojigi'*) is famous the world over and is very convenient, since it can be used for greeting, thanking, leavetaking or apologizing. It can be used when saying "Good morning" (*'ohayō'*), "Hello" (*'konnichiwa'*), "Thank you" (*'arigatō'*), "Goodbye" (*'sayōnara'*) or "Sorry" (*'sumimasen'*).

A man and woman bowing to each other.

Different greetings for different situations:
1) Waving hello to a friend
2) A quick bow in passing
3) A deep, extremely polite bow

Hajimemashité

Shake hands

Business cards (*'meishi'*) can be ordered from local stationers or printers and will usually be ready within a week.

寝る
SLEEPING

These days, many Japanese sleep in beds. However, a much more efficient use of space is obtained with the traditional Japanese sleeping arrangement, which consists of bedding called *'futon'* laid out on the *'tatami'* at night and kept in the closet, or *'oshiiré'*, during the day.

The *'oshiiré'*, a closet with sliding paper doors, is specially-designed for storing *'futon'*. Since Japan is very humid in the summer, it is best to keep the *'futon'* on the upper level of the *'oshiiré'*.

The *'futon'* is very handy – the whole of the floor around it can be used as a bedside table. A complete *'futon'* set consists of a mattress (*'mattoresu'*), under-*futon* (*'shikibuton'*) and sheet (*'shikifu'*) underneath, and a towelling blanket (*'taoruketto'*), ordinary blankets (*'mōfu'*) and an eiderdown (*'kakebuton'*) on top, plus a pillow (*'makura'*) filled with buckwheat chaff (*'sobagara'*) designed to keep the head cool.

You should air your *'futon'* regularly to dry it, and expose it to direct sunlight to kill germs.

USING THE BATH AND TOILET

The Japanese bathroom ('*furoba*') is usually separate from the toilet and looks different from the Western bathroom. It has a tiled floor with taps low down on the wall, and sometimes a shower. The bath itself is square, and is deeper than a Western bath. It is usually filled from a cold tap, and the water is then heated by a gas unit attached to the side.

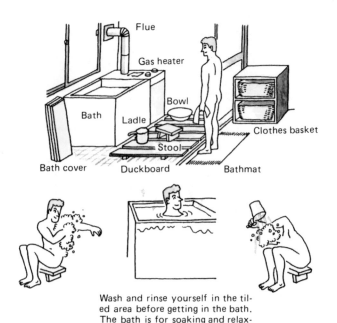

Flue

Gas heater

Bowl

Bath   Ladle

Clothes basket

Bath cover   Duckboard   Bathmat

Stool

Wash and rinse yourself in the tiled area before getting in the bath. The bath is for soaking and relaxing in (that's why it's so hot), and soap, shampoo, etc., should never be used in it.

Japanese-style toilet

Flushing lever

Toilet paper

Both Japanese and Western toilets are used in Japan, and most public lavatories offer a choice. When using a Japanese-style toilet, it is usual to squat facing the hooded end. The Japanese-style toilet is considered by many to be cleaner than the Western-style one because no part of the body comes into contact with it; and for this particular bodily function, squatting is said to be better than sitting.

公衆便所

There is no shortage of public toilets in Japan, but many are not supplied with towels, and some do not have toilet paper. Hot running water is highly unusual. The Japanese habitually carry a handkerchief or tissues for drying the hands.

Some homes in the countryside still do not have flush toilets, and the 'bakyūmu-kā' (honey wagon) is not an unfamiliar sight (or smell).

JAPANESE CLOTHES

Japan's traditional garment, the 'kimono', is well suited to the climate and natural features of the country. However, except on certain formal occasions, the only people who wear 'kimono' nowadays are elderly people and those in certain traditional professions.

Both men and women wear 'kimono' at weddings, and young women often wear them at New Year or at Coming-of-Age ceremonies ('seijin-shiki').

People who normally wear 'kimono':

Traditional comic story-tellers ('rakugoka')

'Sumō' wrestlers ('sumōtori')

Buddhist priests ('obōsan')

Waitresses ('nakai') in traditional Japanese restaurants or hotels ('ryōtei' or 'ryokan')

Japan has four distinct seasons, and the changes in temperature and humidity are large, so make sure you have the right clothes for the right season.

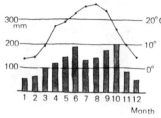

Average temperature and rainfall in Tōkyō

Good grief! It's freezing!

The summer months from June through August are very hot and humid, and schools take their longest holidays during August.

Spring (March through May) and autumn (September through November) are the most comfortable seasons. The rainy season ('*tsuyu*') is in June and July.

Winter is from December to the end of February. The air is very dry, but it is cold enough for snow in most parts of the country, especially in the north.

June

October

An event called *'koromogaé'*, or "change of clothing" takes place throughout Japan in June and October. In June, school pupils change from winter to summer uniform, and businessmen change from dark winter suits to light-colored summer suits. In October, everybody changes back again.

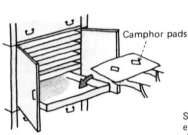

Camphor pads

Storage of *'kimono'*:
1. Fold neatly and put in the special chest called *'tansu'*.
2. Don't forget the camphor pads (*'shōnō'*).

Since the Japanese summer is extremely humid, winter clothes should be aired thoroughly before being put away. Mothballs are a good idea, too.

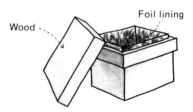

Wood

Foil lining

Japanese tea chests are specially constructed to keep the tea dry, so an empty chest is ideal for storing clothes.

The *'yukata'* is a light cotton *'kimono'*. It is a very simple garment, unlike the *'kimono'* proper, and is a common sight on a summer evening. It is worn by both men and women.

The *'yukata'* is ideal for relaxing in at home, for sleeping in, or for evening strolls. It is sometimes worn with a *'haori'* (half-coat).

Both men and women should wear the *'yukata'* with the left side over the right (right over left is used for dressing corpses). There are no buttons or zips; the *'yukata'* is held together by an *'obi'* or sash. Make sure the *'obi'* is tied neatly, and that the *'yukata'* does not flap open at the front.

Unless you want to be laughed at, wear *'geta'* (high wooden sandals) or *'zōri'* (sandals), not shoes, with your *'yukata'*.

VISITING A JAPANESE HOME

When you visit a Japanese home for the first time, it will make it easier if you know a little about what to do and what not to do before you actually arrive. Many Japanese homes are built in the Western style these days, but the one described here is in the traditional Japanese style.

The gate and front door are usually of the sliding type, and the name of the head of the family (and sometimes those of the whole family) is on a nameplate ('hyōsatsu') outside.

It is good manners to take your coat off before entering the hall.

Take your shoes off in the hall ('genkan') before stepping up into the house.

You will be thought an exceptionally well-mannered guest if you place your shoes tidily together facing back the way you came, as shown in the picture.

The doors to Japanese-style rooms are of the sliding type and consist of a light wooden frame covered with thick, opaque paper on both sides *('fusuma'),* or with semi-transparent paper on one side only *('shōji').* The doorways are rather low, so it is advisable to mind your head when entering or leaving.

Instead of a chair, a cushion *('zabuton')* or a *'zaisu'* (a kind of legless chair) will be offered. Wait until you are invited, and then sit on it in the formal, *'seiza'* position. Sit with your big toes together to prevent your legs from seizing up too quickly.

If another friend or family member is brought into the room, it is good manners to move off the cushion and kneel directly on the *'tatami'* while you are being introduced.

You will soon be invited to relax. Men should then sit cross-legged, and women with their legs together and to one side.

Relaxed position for men *('agura')*

Formal position *('seiza')*

Relaxed position for women

Many homes have a Buddhist altar ('butsudan') containing religious objects and memorial tablets ('ihai') for deceased family members.

Traditional Japanese rooms have a special alcove called 'tokonoma' for the display of flower arrangements, sculptures, hanging scrolls and objets d'art. It is bad manners to stand or sit in this alcove.

Shops, restaurants, martial arts schools and offices also often have a 'kamidana', a kind of miniature Shintō shrine. Elderly people, especially ladies, spend more time praying in front of the 'butsudan' or 'kamidana' than young people, who are usually not very interested in religion.

Houses with gardens often have an 'engawa', or verandah.

This is a pleasant place to sit in the summer, when the tinkling of the 'fūrin', or wind chime, announces that a breeze has come and makes it seem a little cooler.

When visiting someone's home, it is better to avoid mealtimes. However, if you are invited to a meal, don't hesitate to accept.

It's best not to show too much interest in the kitchen, as many Japanese consider this a very private place. Don't worry about helping with the dishes after a meal, either; leave the clearing-away to the hostess.

It is always difficult to know when to leave, especially since politeness requires your hosts to press you to stay a little longer. Green tea will usually be served after the meal, and this can be an indication that it is about time to go.

FINDING ONE'S WAY AROUND

The Japanese address system is rather strange to most Westerners. Tōkyō, for example, is divided into wards, or 'ku', which are then subdivided into 'machi', 'chō-me', 'banchi' and 'gō', each of these being a sub-unit of the one before. The 'gō' number usually designates an individual building.

Except for hills and large avenues, most streets do not have names. This makes it very difficult to find a place even if you know the address, so if you are going somewhere for the first time, you should try and get someone to draw you a map with landmarks before you go.

You will usually find a large map of the area outside stations, showing the 'chōme' and 'banchi' numbers.

You are here.

Look for the 'banchi' numbers on telegraph poles, walls and the gates of houses.

If you get lost, go into the nearest shop and ask the way. The Japanese do this all the time.

Ask at a police box ('*kōban*') if there is one in sight. They always have a detailed map of the area and are happy to give directions.

In country districts, you will find everyone very helpful. Sometimes they will even take you where you want to go.

My name is Satō.

In country villages, many people have the same family name, so make sure you know the full name of the person you are looking for.

電車にのる

TAKING THE TRAIN

The major cities in Japan have highly-developed public transport systems, and the trains are a particularly cheap and convenient means of transport.

The subway systems in big cities such as Tōkyō, Ōsaka and Nagoya are clean, safe and convenient.

Subway entrance

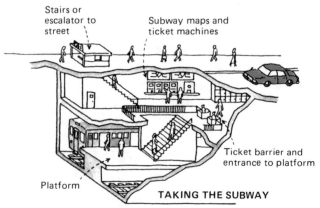

Stairs or escalator to street

Subway maps and ticket machines

Ticket barrier and entrance to platform

Platform

TAKING THE SUBWAY

First, buy your ticket. You can check where you are and where you are going on the subway map near the ticket machines.

Call button

Cancel button

Subway tickets and tickets for local trains are sold by ticket machine.

1 Check the fare to your destination on the fare map.
2 Put the money in the slot.
3 Press the appropriate fare button.
4 Take the ticket and the change.

Most ticket machines accept coins only, although some will take ¥1,000 notes. If you need change and there is no change machine, ask at the ticket office or ticket barrier.

The ticket inspector will punch your ticket as you go in ('kaisa-tsu') and collect it as you leave at your destination.
You can pay any difference in fare at the ticket barrier or at the 'fare adjustment office'.

Put your ticket in the slot.

The gate will open and you can take your ticket.

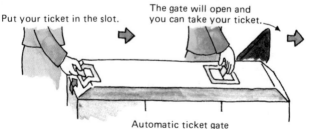

Automatic ticket gate

The crowding in Japanese trains is notorious. During the morning and evening rush hours, the trains and subways are sometimes packed to more than three times their specified capacity.

Special pushers, called 'oshiya', force the people in so the doors can close.

Beep! Get back behind the white line, please!

Taped announcements in Japanese give a constant stream of information and warnings.

HOW TO BE A MODEL PASSENGER

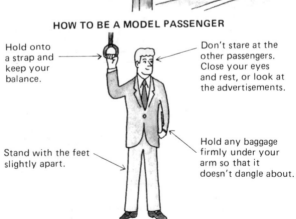

Hold onto a strap and keep your balance.

Don't stare at the other passengers. Close your eyes and rest, or look at the advertisements.

Stand with the feet slightly apart.

Hold any baggage firmly under your arm so that it doesn't dangle about.

BAD MANNERS ON THE TRAIN

Holding a newspaper wide open so it hits other passengers in the face.

Sitting with the legs spread out as if relaxing at home.

Smoking (smoking is prohibited in subways and on subway platforms at all time).

Falling asleep on another passenger's shoulder.

Taking up more than one space on the seat.

Accidentally allowing the hands to wander in the direction of female passengers.

USING THE MUNICIPAL BUSES

Once you have become familiar with the trains and subways, you might like to try the buses. It will give you a new perspective on city life as you gaze through the windows.

Bus stations usually have an information desk where you can find out which bus you need. You can also buy books of tickets ('*kaisūken*') here at a reduced rate.

Most buses are one-man operated, and the fare is usually a standard fixed value in the cities, no matter how far you travel. You put the fare in the fare box next to the driver's seat when you board the bus.

The fare box will give change automatically for coins, but not for notes, so make sure you have some small change before you get on the bus.

28

Japanese roads are often very crowded, and the bus will stop and start a lot, so it's best to hold onto something while the bus is moving.

Some buses have a low roof at the back, so mind your head.

Tsugi wa Omotesandō desu

The driver plays taped announcements telling you the name of the next stop and giving various warnings and other information. Press the buzzer if you want the bus to stop.

If you are not sure of being able to recognize your stop when you come to it, ask the driver when you get on the bus.

TAKING A TAXI

Taxis can easily be picked up at hotel and station taxi stands, or you can hail one in the street by raising your hand.

Taxi stand

All taxis have a sign on the roof.

Hey, taxi

IN THE STREET

Empty taxis display a red light inside the windscreen on the passenger's side. This light is green if the taxi is occupied.

It's sometimes very difficult to get a taxi to stop late at night in the entertainment districts.

Passengers usually ride in the back unless there are too many to squeeze in. The back doors are opened and closed automatically by the driver, so remember to stand clear of them.

It's a good thing to make a habit of taking one of the taxi company's namecards when you get in a taxi. Then, if you leave something in the taxi, you will be able to trace it easily.

You can transport luggage in the boot of a taxi without having to pay any extra money.

Pay the fare shown on the meter when you arrive at your destination, before you get out of the taxi. A surcharge is added between 11 p.m. and 5 a.m., or if you have called the taxi by telephone. No tip is needed.

Most taxi drivers speak no English, so either practise the correct pronunciation of your destination or get someone to write it for you in Japanese. Also, don't expect the driver to know how to get to where you want to go. Unless it's a very well-known place, you will probably have to give directions.

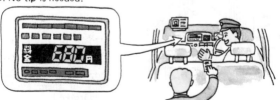

車を運転する

DRIVING

Driving in Japan is a tricky business. The roads are very narrow and crowded and the signs are hard to understand. Car rental is popular and you can easily hire a car or truck if you have an international driving licence, but it is probably best to wait until you are used to the country before attempting to do this. It might also be a good idea to ask a Japanese friend to ride with you, at least until you get to know your way around.

There are plenty of road signs, but signs giving information are mostly in Japanese and symbols.

Driving in Japan is on the left, as in the U.K. and some other countries. Japanese cars are right-hand drive.

It's best to stick to the major roads when driving in Japan. The back streets are narrow and difficult to negotiate, and many of them are one-way ('ippōtsūkō').

Traffic jams are a common sight on Japanese roads, especially during the morning and evening rush hours in the city, and on Saturday and Sunday on the highway.

Display showing the length of the traffic jam ahead.

Small scooters and mini-bikes are very popular, and their riders are often inexperienced. Car and truck drivers should keep a good look-out for them and for pedestrians.

The police often set up speed traps, a practice known as *'nezumi-tori'*, or "rat-catching". Speed limits are rather low (40 kph in cities), and not many people actually observe them.

Drunk drivers are dealt with very harshly in Japan. Anyone suspected of driving while under the influence is breathalysed, and they will lose their licence if the test is positive. Spot checks are also common.

If you have an accident or breakdown while on a motorway, you can summon help from one of the many roadside emergency telephones.

The Japan Automobile Federation (JAF) is equivalent to the American Automobile Association (AAA) and will assist you if you have any troubles.

The Japanese are not very well-mannered drivers, especially when it comes to throwing rubbish out of the car windows.

This green-and-yellow symbol, in the shape of a leaf ('*shoshinsha-māku*'), shows that the driver has only recently passed the driving test.

Take care when driving in cities, since people are liable to pop out from side streets without warning.

Female traffic wardens drive around in little police cars looking for illegally-parked vehicles. When they find one, they mark the position of the vehicle's wheels with a piece of chalk on the end of a long stick.

Illegal parking is quite common in the cities, since it is often hard to find a place to park. If a car is left illegally-parked for too long, the traffic wardens will call the towaway truck to take it away.

RENTING ACCOMMODATION

Anyone staying in Japan for any length of time will have to rent a flat or house. Flats in Japan are called *'apāto'* (cheaper, often of wooden construction, in a small apartment block or house) or *'manshon'* (more expensive, usually in a larger, modern, ferroconcrete apartment building).

You can find flats and houses advertised in newspapers or magazines (some magazines are devoted entirely to lists of accommodation for rent), or you can go to the location of your choice and look in estate agents' windows.

Always inspect your new home carefully before renting it. Check such things as the layout of the rooms, the amount of sunlight the place receives, and the quietness and convenience (or otherwise) of the neighbourhood, and don't hesitate to turn a place down if you don't like it.

When you have decided on a place, you will have to go to the estate agent's office to sign (or seal) the contract and hand over the money. You will usually have to pay one or two months' 'key money'('*reikin*') to the landlord('*ōya*'), one month's agent's fee('*tesūryō*') to the agent, two or three months' refundable deposit ('*shikikin*') and one month's rent ('*yachin*') in advance, so you will need to have at least six times the monthly rent in your pocket, and sometimes more.

rent in advance

deposit

key money & agent's fee

If you are moving from one flat to another, the cheapest way is to hire a lorry and do the job yourself, with the aid of friends.

If this is too difficult, you can engage the services of a removal firm. Some of these offer a comprehensive service which includes packing and unpacking.

USING THE TELEPHONE

Japan is well equipped with public telephones ('*Kōshū-denwa*'), especially around stations and shopping areas. They come in a variety of colors–red, yellow, pink, and green, etc.

HOW TO USE THE PUBLIC TELEPHONE

Lift the receiver and put a ¥10 or ¥100 coin in the slot. Red and pink phones accept only ¥10 coins, while yellow and green phones take both ¥10 and ¥100 coins. You can put in up to six coins at a time.

Dial the number.

You will hear a buzzer tone when your money is about to run out. Put another coin in quickly if you want to continue talking. Local calls cost ¥10 for one minute.

A telephone card might be handy if you do a lot of phoning from outside. Telephone cards are accepted by green telephones, some of which also take ¥10 and ¥100 coins. Don't forget to dial the area code if you are making a call from one area to another.

Telephone cards can be bought at shops displaying this sign.

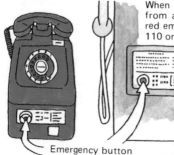

When making an emergency call from a public telephone, press the red emergency button and then dial 110 or 119. No money is needed.

Emergency button

EMERGENCY NUMBERS

Police: 110
Fire and ambulance: 119

A travel information and assistance service in English is available for foreign tourists. The number is 3502-1461 in Tōkyō and 371-5649 in Kyōto. Outside these cities, in eastern Japan dial 0088-22-2800, and in western Japan dial 0088-22-4800 (both toll-free).

INTERNATIONAL CALLS

International calls may be made from the green international and domestic card/coin telephones with a golden-olive panel. These phones also handle international direct dialing calls, collect calls and international credit calls.
Collect calls, Credit calls: 0051

If you want a telephone installed in your flat when you first move in, the estate agent will arrange it for you. Otherwise, ask someone (e.g. your landlord) to help you, or go to the telephone office yourself.

SENDING MAIL

A lot of business and private communication in Japan is carried out by telephone, but letters are still sent to convey personal greetings or detailed information.

You don't have to be able to write Japanese to get a letter delivered, either in Japan or to an address abroad. Addresses in the Roman alphabet will be understood, provided they are written clearly and correctly.

Post boxes in major cities usually have two slots. The left-hand one is for ordinary letters and postcards, while the right-hand one is for letters to overseas addresses and express delivery letters. There are usually four or five collections a day.

The old-style red pillar boxes can still be seen in some local districts.

Can I open a current account?

Post offices in Japan are indicated by the symbol 〒. Besides handling all types of mail, they can also transfer money by telephone or telegram, and accept payment of tax, telephone, electricity, national health and other government bills. They even administer savings and pensions. Stamps and postcards can be bought at post offices or at shops displaying the 〒(post office) mark.

* Symbol of a delivery service agency ('Takuhaibin').

There are many private door-to-door delivery services which you can use for small parcels or large items such as furniture. These will deliver speedily to anywhere in Japan. Local rice merchants, off-licences and other businesses often operate as agents for these services.

The New Year's card ('nengajō') is one of the most important greeting cards in Japan (another is 'shochū-mimai', or an "inquiry after your health in the hot season"). All the New Year's cards posted before about the middle of December are kept back by the post office, and are delivered all at once on New Year's morning by hordes of students acting as temporary postmen.

KEEPING UP WITH THE NEWS

Japan boasts the biggest circulation of newspapers of any country in the world. Besides the Japan Times, there are other English-language newspapers put out by each of the big newspaper companies, *Asahi, Mainichi* and *Yomiuri.*

Newspapers are available at station newsstands and hotel bookshops.

Major foreign newspapers and magazines can be bought at hotels or large bookshops, or you can go to a library and read them.

If you move into a flat or house, you won't have to wait long before a newspaper salesman comes knocking on the door. If you want to have a paper delivered, just sign up on the spot.

Your paper will be delivered every day, and someone will come to collect the money at the end of each month. No tip or commission is required, and you can cancel your subscription at any time.

Half the readers of English-language newspapers in Japan are Japanese, and they are very interested in what foreign residents and visitors have to say. So don't hesitate to write to your favourite paper and express your opinions.

The American Forces' Far East Network (FEN) is an English-language radio service that can be heard anywhere in Japan. If you have a multiplex television, you can also get the news in English and listen to the original soundtracks of many foreign films.

USING THE BANK

Anyone staying in Japan for any length of time will have to learn how to use the banks. Opening times are 9:00 a.m. to 3:00 p.m. Monday to Friday. All the banks are closed on Saturdays, Sundays and public holidays.

Most banks have a foreign exchange counter, but some local banks do not offer this service.

Some banks require you to have a 'hanko' (personal seal) when opening an account, and will not accept a signature.

If you can't find the counter you are looking for, ask one of the attendants who walk around keeping the place tidy and answering inquiries.

The ¥1,000, ¥5,000 and ¥10,000 banknotes were changed in November, 1984. The old notes are still legal tender.

1 yen

5 yen

10 yen

50 yen

100 yen

500 yen

The ¥10 and ¥100 coins are the most useful, since they can be used in both telephones and automatic vending machines.

1,000 yen

Natumé Sōseki
(1867-1916)
Novelist and critic of the *Meiji* period.

5,000 yen

Nitobé Inazō
(1862-1933)
Educator of the *Meiji* and *Taishō* periods.

10,000 yen

Fukuzawa Yukichi
(1835-1901)
Enlightenment thinker of the *Meiji* period.

HOW TO USE A CASH DISPENSER

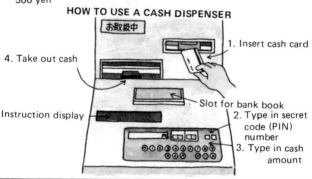

お取扱中

1. Insert cash card

4. Take out cash

Slot for bank book

Instruction display

2. Type in secret code (PIN) number

3. Type in cash amount

SHOPPING

For shopping, there's a choice of department stores, super-markets or speciality shops. Once you get to know them, you'll find out which is best for a particular type of shopping.

Department stores have a wide range of goods including top-quality, expensive items. Super-markets sell mainly food and other daily necessities.

The food floor in department stores is usually in the basement. You can pick up some bargains if you go there just before closing time.

Many department stores and supermarkets offer free tasting of certain products('*shishoku*'). You can almost make a meal by walking round and trying them all.

There is no bargaining in Japan, except at special places like Aki-habara. Prices are almost always fixed.

Most shops have electronic cash registers. Even at shops that don't have these, service is usually fast and efficient.

More and more department stores are allowing the use of credit cards.

Department stores hold sales about twice a year, when they are descended on by hordes of women and turn into veritable battlefields.

売りつくしバーゲン

Arigatō gozaimashita.

Some department stores have their staff line up and bow to the first customers entering at opening time and the last customers leaving at closing time.

Anyone who wants to find a bargain should go to one of the many discount shops, such as the camera shops near Shinjuku Station in Tokyo. These shops buy their goods in quantity at low prices and sell them cheaply.

Pawn shops ('*Shichiya*') used to be popular places where one could buy a wide range of second-hand goods cheaply. They are not so popular these days, however.

Anyone who visits Tōkyō will soon hear of Akihabara, Japan's electrical and electronic goods paradise. Both finished goods and parts can be bought here, and this is one of the few places in Japan where you can bargain.

Besides department stores and supermarkets, there are many small shops specializing in a particular line of goods. It's better to buy fresh fish at a fishmonger's ('sakanaya') or fresh vegetables at a greengrocer's ('yaoya') than frozen goods at a supermarket.

Most shops close at about seven p.m., though some stay open later. There are quite a few convenience stores that are open twenty-four hours a day.

When all the shops are closed, you can sometimes find what you want in one of the many automatic vending machines on the streets. They sell mainly cigarettes, drinks (including alcohol) and magazines.

Automatic ➡ vending machines ('jidō-hanbaiki')

EATING OUT

It's easy to eat cheaply and well in Japan if you know where to go; and in the cities, you can find all kinds of food from all over the world.

Japanese restaurants usually hang a short curtain called *'noren'* outside when they are open for meals, and take it in when they close.

Many restaurants offer low-priced set meals (*'teishoku'*) at lunchtime, which is usually from noon to 2 p.m. for office workers; and the more popular places soon fill up with people taking advantage of this.

A Japanese set meal consists of a main dish such as grilled fish (a), a bowl of rice (b), a bowl of *'miso'* soup (c), and a small dish of pickles (d).

Some cheap restaurants called *'teishokuya'* sell these items separately, so you can make up your own combination. Sometimes you serve yourself, and sometimes you buy tickets and give them to the waitress when she takes your order. These restaurants are popular among students.

If you cannot read the menu and don't know how to order, either take the waitress outside and point to one of the plastic food models, or simply order what someone else is eating.

Some restaurants serve a variety of food; Japanese, Chinese, French, Italian, etc., but most specialize in a particular kind. You will get special service if you become a regular customer (*'jōren'*) at a particular restaurant.

Many people save money by bringing a lunch box *('bentō')* to work and eating it at their desk. A *'bentō'* consists of rice, pickles, fish, meat, etc. packed in a handy box and carried in a bag or wrapped in a cloth.

Many offices and factories have their own dining halls. These are often self-service, and are cheap, since they are usually subsidised by the company.

Omachidōsama !

People who haven't brought a lunch box and are too busy to leave their desk can order meals by telephone from local restaurants. This service is called *'demaé'* and is very common in Japan. Housewives use the service too, and the delivery boy on bicycle or motorbike is a familiar sight.

Many American fast-food companies have set up operation in Japan, so if you get tired of Japanese food, you can easily find a place to get hamburgers or fried chicken.

The *'bentōya'* is a kind of Japanese fast-food store where you can choose from a selection of hot and cold boxed lunches to take away with you.

If you are in a hurry, you can eat standing up at one of the many *'tachigui'* (literally, "standing-eating") restaurants to be found in and around stations. These places serve cheap dishes such as *'soba'* and *'udon'*(Japanese noodles), or *'rāmen'*(Chinese noodles).

TEA, COFFEE AND JAPANESE TEA

Tea *('kōcha')* and coffee *('kōhī')* are very popular in Japan, and are served at the ubiquitous *'kissaten'* (cafés). However, if you make a business call or visit someone's home, you will probably be offered Japanese tea, or *'ocha'*. This is usually pale green and is served without milk, sugar or lemon, in cups without handles.

There are many different types and grades of Japanese tea. The three main types are *'sencha'*, which is green, *'bancha'*, which is light brown, and *'matcha'*, the powdered green tea used in the tea ceremony.

HOW TO MAKE A GOOD CUP OF TEA

1. Heat both the pot and the teacups.
2. Boil the water and allow it to cool to the correct temperature before pouring it onto the tea-leaves in the pot. The temperature of the water and the time for which the tea should be left to stand before serving depend on the type and grade of tea used.

HOW TO DRINK JAPANESE TEA

1. If the teacup has a lid, place the lid upside down to the right of the teacup.

2. Use two hands to hold the cup, with one hand underneath, and drink the tea quietly.

3. If a Japanese cake *('wagashi')* is served with the tea, cut it with the bamboo stick provided and eat it piece by piece.

Cafés in Japan are used for meeting friends, passing the time, or conducting business. A cup of tea or coffee may seem expensive, but you can stay in the café as long as you like and will not be pressured to leave or order more when you have finished.

Irasshaimasé. Nanni nasai masuka ?

Service in cafés is usually very good. You will be given a glass of water and sometimes an *'oshibori'* (wet towel) when you enter. A small clipboard with your bill attached will be placed on your table, and you pay at the desk when you leave. No tips are needed.

Most cafés only offer single cups of tea or coffee; a pot of tea or a 'bottomless cup' of coffee is hard to find. However, many cafés offer a bargain breakfast, called *'mōningu sābisu'*, consisting of coffee or tea, a boiled egg, toast and butter, and sometimes a small salad.

PASSING THE TIME IN CAFÉS

If you have time to kill, you can go to a café and read a book or a newspaper; nobody will object. Most cafés have a rack with comic books, papers and magazines.
Some cafés have TV games built into the tables.

Some cafés specialize in jazz, rock, classical and other types of music. Many of these cafés will play customers' requests.

The traditional Japanese café is the *'kammikissa'*. These serve Japanese tea and various kinds of Japanese sweets and cakes.

You can often buy Japanese cakes to take away.

Like restaurants, *'kammikissa'* usually have wax models of the food outside.

'Kammikissa' are popular with ladies. Men sometimes take their girl friends to them, but do not often go to them alone.

If you have a sweet tooth, you might like to try the traditional Japanese desserts *'ammitsu'* and *'oshiruko'.* *'Kakigōri'* (shaved ice with flavoured syrup) is popular in summer.

oshiruko

ammitsu

kakigōri

酒をのむ
DRINKING

Japan is full of drinking places *('nomiya')*. All kinds of alcohol are available, but the most popular are *'saké'*, *'shōchū'* (a spirit distilled from grain, sweet potatoes, etc.), beer and whisky.

"Let's go and have a drink"

This action represents drinking. It is used when inviting someone to go for a drink.

Most ordinary Japanese steer clear of high-class bars and nightclubs unless they are entertaining on the company expense account.

58

The average company worker goes drinking at economically-priced beer halls, 'robatayaki' (Japanese-style pubs serving a wide range of food), 'yakitoriya' (pubs specializing in 'yakitori') and other kinds of 'izakaya', or drinking establishment. The Japanese like to take their dinner as a succession of snacks while drinking, often ending up with a rice dish such as 'ochazuké' (a kind of rice soup).

Tsugi é ikō, tsugi é

A popular Japanese pastime is 'hashigozaké' (pub-crawling). Instead of relaxing in one place, everybody will suddenly get up, crying 'tsugi ni ikimashō' ("Let's go") and rush out, leaving their drinks unfinished. Going along with them will help cement relationships and make them feel you are more like "one of them".

The Japanese like to drink in groups. It is bad form to start drinking as soon as your glass is filled. When everyone is ready, everybody shouts 'kanpai' ("bottoms up") and starts swigging.

Most Japanese turn red after taking a little alcohol. After a lot, they get happily or sentimentally drunk, but not usually violently drunk. Sometimes they get noisy and sometimes sick, but all this is looked on benevolently in Japan; being drunk excuses behaviour that would otherwise be frowned on.

If someone offers to fill your *'saké'* cup, you should first knock back what is in it before proffering the empty cup to be filled. Unless things are very informal, everyone fills each other's glasses or cups rather than their own.

When drinking in groups, everyone usually pays an equal share of the bill, rather than bothering to work out what each individual has had. This system is called *'warikan'* (going Dutch).

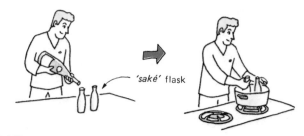

'saké' flask

'Saké' is usually warmed and drunk neat. If you are drinking at home, put the 'saké' into a 'tokkuri' ('saké' flask) and stand it in boiling water until the neck of the flask becomes almost too hot to hold. To order hot 'saké' when drinking out, ask for 'atsukan'. Cold 'saké' ('hiyazaké') is best drunk from the small square wooden boxes called 'masu', with a pinch of salt on the corner of the box.

'Shōchū'   Hot water

Another popular Japanese drink is 'shōchū', a spirit distilled from grain, sweet potatoes, etc. It is usually drunk with hot water ('oyuwari') or with soda and lemon ('chūhai').

Umeboshi

kaki

Ochazuké
(rice soup)

'Ochazuké' (rice soup), 'kaki' (persimmons) and 'umeboshi' (salted plums) are supposed to be good for preventing hangovers ('futsuka-yoi'). An 'umeboshi' mashed in a cup of green tea the morning after is particularly revitalizing.

銭湯へいく

USING THE PUBLIC BATH

The institution of the public bath ('*sentō*') has died out in most Western countries, but it is still hanging on, for the time being, in Japan. If you don't visit one at least once, then you cannot be said to know Japan.

soap shampoo   hand
      ('*shampū*') towel

Wear casual clothes (some people go in pyjamas!) and leave your valuables at home.

Put your soap ('*sekken*'), flannel and other washing gear in a small plastic washbowl ('*semmenki*') and tuck it under your arm.

SENTŌ STYLE

You can identify the '*sentō*' by its tall chimney with the special '*sentō*' mark. These chimneys are a standard 23 meters high.

Leave your shoes in one of the lockers in the entrance and go in the men's or women's door as appropriate. You pay the attendant ('*bandai*') in advance, and strip off in the changing area. You may encounter a few surreptitious stares, but this is perfectly natural. Simply ignore them.

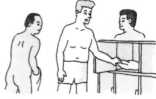

Put your clothes in one of the free lockers provided.

The locker key will jump out when you push in the small lever on the right of the lock.

Put the key around your wrist so as not to lose it.

Always wash and rinse yourself before getting in the bathtub. Never get in the bath with soap on you.

Sit on one of the little plastic stools when washing yourself, and take care not to splash your neighbours.

There are usually two separate tubs, one very hot and one super-hot.

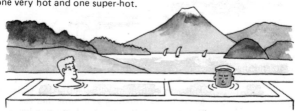

Many 'sentō' have a picture of the sea and Mount Fuji on the wall behind the bathtub. You can use this to help you imagine you are floating in the ocean.

BARBERS AND HAIRDRESSERS

Barbers' shops (*'rihatsuten'* or *'tokoya'*) are easy to find in Japan. Just look for the red, white and blue pole, the same as in Western countries.

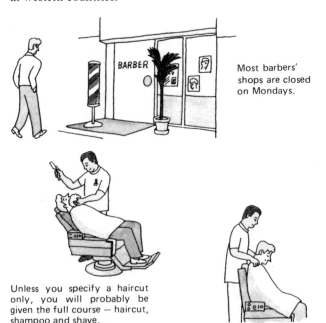

Most barbers' shops are closed on Mondays.

Unless you specify a haircut only, you will probably be given the full course — haircut, shampoo and shave.

Japanese barbers are very painstaking, and many go as far as trimming your nose and ear hairs. Hot face towels and a head and shoulder massage are included in the price at some places, extra at others.

Women have a wide choice of hairdressers ranging from ordinary local places to fashionably-designed, up-to-the-minute modern beauty parlours.

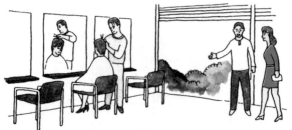

"All right, I'll be there at six."

Most hairdressers are closed on Tuesdays.

It's best to make an appointment so as to avoid a long wait.

Most hairdressers provide magazines for their customers, and some even serve tea.

Many Japanese ladies wear *kimono* at New Year, and some have their hair done in the traditional Japanese style to go with it. Hairdressers are therefore unusually crowded at this time.
Manicures and make-up are also available at some establishments.

洗濯物を出す

GOING TO THE CLEANERS

There is no shortage of small cleaning shops in Japan. Prices and times vary a little, as does the quality of the cleaning, so it's best to shop around.

Most places ask their customers to pay for the cleaning when they hand the dirty clothes in.

When you have paid, you will get a receipt and a list of the items to be cleaned. That's a good time to check when the cleaning will be ready.

Don't forget to take your receipt and list with you when you go to pick up the cleaning.

Many cleaners these days do not do the cleaning themselves. They simply collect it and send it off to a central cleaning depot.

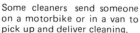

Some cleaners send someone on a motorbike or in a van to pick up and deliver cleaning.

Make sure you give the cleaners any special instructions needed. Some cleaners provide special services such as spot cleaning, cleaning of down or leather garments, and mending.

PUTTING OUT THE RUBBISH

Cities in Japan have a well-regulated system for rubbish collection, and if you live here, you will have to learn the rules unless you want to make yourself unpopular with the neighbours.

Always have two separate bags or boxes handy (you can buy plastic rubbish bags at any supermarket). One of these is for burnable rubbish (such as paper, cardboard or food scraps)('*moeru gomi*'), and the other is for non-burnable rubbish (such as empty cans and bottles)('*moenai gomi*'), or anything which gives off poisonous vapour when burnt.

Find your nearest rubbish collection point and check the sign telling you the collection days. Make sure you put out the right kind of rubbish on the right day, and never put any out on non-collection days.

Collection times vary, but it is best to put out the rubbish between eight and nine in the morning to make sure of catching the cart.

The ordinary rubbish cart cannot take large items ('*sodaigomi*') such as furniture. Some areas have a regular day for collecting this kind of rubbish, while in some areas, you have to telephone and ask them to come.

This service ('*chirigami-kōkan*') is provided by private operators who tour the neighbourhood in small trucks with loudspeakers.

Maido onajimino chirigami kōkan desu

'Chirigami-kōkan'

If you save your old newspapers and magazines separately, you can exchange them for tissue paper or toilet paper.

GOING TO HOSPITAL

Medical care in Japan is of a high standard, and there are large numbers of major hospitals and smaller clinics.

There is no 'family doctor' system in Japan, so you are free to go to any clinic you like.

General hospitals do not usually accept appointments for outpatient treatment. Since they can be very crowded, it's best to telephone and check the situation before you go.

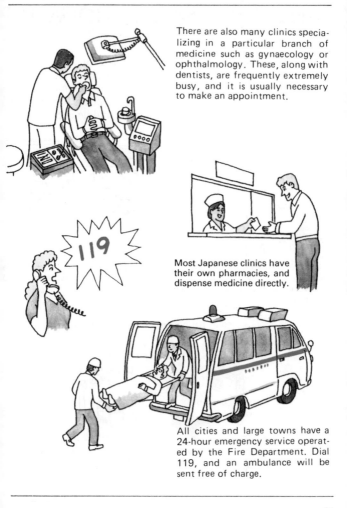

There are also many clinics specializing in a particular branch of medicine such as gynaecology or ophthalmology. These, along with dentists, are frequently extremely busy, and it is usually necessary to make an appointment.

Most Japanese clinics have their own pharmacies, and dispense medicine directly.

All cities and large towns have a 24-hour emergency service operated by the Fire Department. Dial 119, and an ambulance will be sent free of charge.

TYPHOONS AND EARTHQUAKES

If you live in Japan, you should be prepared for the occasional typhoon or earthquake. Typhoons are tropical depressions produced in the South Pacific. They sometimes move north and hit Japan, usually 9 – 10 days after being formed. The typhoon season is from late August to the middle of September.

Listen out for typhoon warnings on the radio or television, and make sure you fix any damage to your flat or house.

Flooding often occurs near the sea or rivers, and you may be forced to evacuate.

Your basic emergency kit should include the following items:

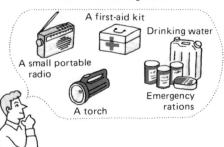

A first-aid kit

Drinking water

A small portable radio

A torch

Emergency rations

Earthquakes are quite frequent in Japan (legend has it that they are caused by a giant *'namazu'* (catfish) wiggling its tail under the earth), and they can be frightening if you are not used to them. If an earthquake occurs while you are at home, here is what you should do:

1. Turn off gas and electrical appliances such as cookers, fires, bath, etc. Turn off all the gas taps.

2. Open a door or window so you can get out after the earthquake has stopped. (Door and window frames can warp and jam, trapping you inside. Don't run outside in a panic; you might get hit by falling glass or other objects.

3. Get under a table or other protection and listen to the emergency bulletins on the radio. Earthquakes don't last long, although the aftershocks can continue for some time. Wait for the quake to finish before leaving cover.

日本料理を作る

COOKING JAPANESE FOOD

Japanese food not only has a unique taste, it also uses unique methods of cooking and unique ingredients. Why not try preparing a few simple Japanese dishes, making sure that you use ingredients that are in season *('shun')*?

SPRING: *'fuki'* (bog rhubarb)

SUMMER: *'awabi'* (abalone)
'momo' (peach)

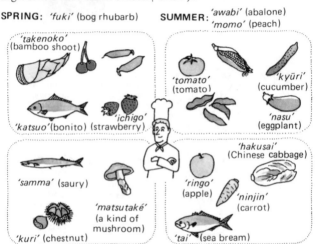

'takenoko' (bamboo shoot)

'katsuo' (bonito) *'ichigo'* (strawberry)

'tomato' (tomato)

'kyūri' (cucumber)

'nasu' (eggplant)

'samma' (saury)

'matsutaké' (a kind of mushroom)

'kuri' (chestnut)

'hakusai' (Chinese cabbage)

'ringo' (apple)

'ninjin' (carrot)

'tai' (sea bream)

AUTUMN: *'nashi'* (Japanese pear)
'kaki' (persimmon)

WINTER: *'daikon'* (Japanese radish)
'mikan' (tangerine)

Basic cutting methods: In Japanese cooking, appearance is almost as important as taste. The ingredients are cut in different ways to suit a particular dish.

'kazarikiri' (decorative cut)

'sengiri' (julienne cut)

'mijingiri' (chopped fine)

Sushi is not too difficult to make at home — just try and copy your local *sushi* chef.

Hold the topping *('neta')* in your left hand and apply a dab of *'wasabi'* (Japanese horseradish).

Take some vinegar-flavoured *sushi* rice *('shari')* in your right hand and squeeze it lightly into an oblong shape.

Don't forget to put some vinegar on your hands before you start, or you will have very sticky fingers.

Place the rice on top of the topping in your left hand and press it with the fingers of the right hand.

Turn the *sushi* with the topping the right way up and press into shape.

Even if it doesn't look very professional, home-made *sushi* always seems to taste good.

Natural food is becoming more and more popular in Japan. Here are some simple dishes that you can add to your repertoire.

Brown rice ('gemmai') is packed with vitamins and calcium. It is harder than white rice and is best cooked in a pressure-cooker, but an ordinary pot with weights on will do.

Tōfu is a health food made from soybeans, which have been dubbed 'meat in vegetable farm' because of their high protein content.

Use a spoon to scoop out a shallow hollow in the top of the 'tōfu', and put the condiments in this together with a little soy sauce.

The simplest way of eating tōfu is in the form of 'hiyayakko'. This dish also allows you to appreciate the true taste of tōfu. To prepare it, chill a block of tōfu and prepare some 'yakumi' (condiments) such as grated ginger ('oroshi shōga') and chopped chives ('asatsuki').

A RECIPE FOR 'AGEDASHI-DŌFU' (fried 'tōfu')

Cut a block of 'tōfu' in two and cover it in a thick layer of flour.

Fry it in oil at 160 – 170°C until it turns golden brown.

Usually eaten in katsuo-bushi soup.

Sukiyaki is easy to cook — in fact, it is cooked at the table. It's a good dish for parties.

First, buy some thinly-sliced beef and a selection of vegetables in season, together with some *yakidōfu* (broiled *tōfu*) and some *'shirataki'* (noodles made from devil's-tongue starch).

beef

shirataki

yakidōfu

vegetables

Cut the ingredients into bite-sized pieces and arrange them artistically on a large plate.

soy sauce

sugar

mirin

saké

Heat a little oil in a pan or on a hot plate, and fry the beef lightly. Then add the rest of the ingredients together with some stock made from soy sauce, *'mirin'* (sweet rice wine), sugar and *'saké'*, and wait until the food is cooked.

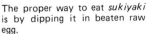

The proper way to eat *sukiyaki* is by dipping it in beaten raw egg.

STUDYING JAPANESE

Japanese is a very interesting language, and more and more people are studying it these days. The number of Japanese language schools at home and abroad is increasing steadily.

Japanese may seem difficult to start with, but if you persist, you will soon be able to make yourself understood. You can get by in Japan speaking only English, but if you don't learn Japanese, you will be missing a lot.

Language exchange is one way to learn Japanese. You can find a language-exchange partner through advertisements in newspapers or notices on message boards, or by visiting one of the many "English-speaking coffee shops".

A good way to start familiarizing yourself with the Japanese writing system is to study shop signs, street signs and other signboards. Station signs are helpful, because they are often written in 'kanji' (Chinese characters, extensively used in Japanese), 'hiragana' (one of the two Japanese syllabaries, the other being 'katakana'), and the Roman alphabet.

Unlike adults, children are often not shy about talking to foreigners — and they don't become tongue-tied through thinking that they have to speak in English.

If you are not very fond of children, you can try chatting to students or older school pupils. They all study English at school and are eager to talk to foreigners. Another good way, though a bit hard on the liver, is to frequent cheap bars and talk to the locals.

If you want to study Japanese properly, you will have to enrol in the Japanese studies department of a university or find a private school, of which there are plenty.

USEFUL JAPANESE EXPRESSIONS

If you are starting to learn Japanese, you will soon realize that the following expressions can be used in a wide variety of different situations. It is worth listening for them and making them part of your vocabulary.

☆ *Dōmo* (literal meaning: "very")

This is used to intensify expressions such as "*arigatō*" ("thank you") and "*sumimasen*"("thank you" or "I'm sorry"). It can also be used on its own to mean "thanks" or "sorry", or even "hello" or "goodbye".

☆ *Chotto* (literal meaning: "a little")

This word is commonly heard in the expression "*chotto matté*"("wait just a moment"). It expresses reservation in "*chotto sumimasen*"("excuse me a moment") and "*chotto muzukashii*" ("I'm afraid that would be a little difficult"). It can also be used on its own instead of "*sumimasen*" to attract a waiter's attention in a restaurant.

☆ *Ii desu* (literal meaning: "that's fine").

This expression is confusing, since it can have two diametrically opposite meanings, as in "*kōhī wa ikaga desu ka*?"("would you like some coffee?") "*Ii desu*"("Yes, please" or "No, thank you"). The meanings are discriminated by gesture or facial expression.

ENJOYING

GETTING ON WITH THE JAPANESE

The best way of getting friendly with the Japanese is to learn a little of their language. They will feel a lot closer to you if you can speak even a little.

Most Japanese have studied English for at least six years at school and college. However, most of this study consists of reading or studying grammar, with almost no conversation practice.

When speaking English, you should therefore try to speak slowly and clearly, in short sentences. If you cannot make yourself understood, try writing down what you want to say.

Would you speak more slowly, please?

Ooh! What style!

Most Japanese would love to be seen conversing fluently with a foreigner. Even a brief conversation, if successful, will make them very happy.

"Come and visit my house sometime" (meaning: "I think you're quite a good fellow")

When you first meet the Japanese, you may be surprised at how reticent they are about expressing their own desires and opinions. You may also notice a considerable gap between what they say and what they actually mean.

"I'll consider it carefully and let you know one way or the other" (meaning: "You'll have to come up with something better than that")

"Let's have a drink together next time we meet" (meaning: "I wouldn't mind having a drink with you if we happen to get the chance sometime or other")

You may find the Japanese hard to get along with at first, but once you make friends with them, you will find you are treated very kindly.

Many Japanese show modesty by deprecating themselves and flattering others. This is considered a very desirable trait in Japan.

カラオケで歌う
SINGING TO KARAOKÉ

'Karaoké' is a form of entertainment that has recently become so popular in Japan that regulations have had to be passed to control the noise it creates. The word *'karaoké'* comes from *'kara'*, meaning "empty" plus *'oké'*, short for "orchestra". In it, tapes are played with backing music but no words, and people sing the words in time to the music, using a microphone.

People enjoy this pastime at home or in one of the many *'karaoké'* bars that have proliferated in recent years.

The usual *'karaoké'* songs are *'enka'*, or popular ballads. They have distinctive Japanese melodies, and the words are often very sentimental.

84

Japanese businessmen love *'karaoké'*. Sometimes, when they have had a bit too much to drink, they even argue over whose turn it is for the microphone.

The people listening tolerate a poor singer and applaud a good one. There are even private *'karaoké'* schools where you can go to polish your performance.

If you live in Japan, you will sooner or later be taken to a *'karaoké'* bar and asked to perform, so it's a wise move to learn a couple of songs ahead of time.

Most *'karaoké'* bars have some Western songs among their tapes; 'Yesterday' and 'My Way' are big favourites. The Japanese usually sing with the words in front of them, and the songbooks sometimes have the lyrics in English.

PLAYING PACHINKO

'Pachinko', a kind of vertical pinball game, is one of the most popular amusements in Japan. You can easily recognize a 'pachinko' parlour by its bright fluorescent lighting and loud music, and the incessant noise of the machines.

HOW TO PLAY

1. First get some 'pachinko' balls from the ball machine.
2. Take the balls to a machine in one of the plastic boxes provided.
3. Pour the balls into the feed chute and turn the automatic handle to the right to shoot.

When a ball lands in one of the catchers, the machine will reward you with more balls. If you strike lucky and exhaust the machine's supply of balls, the *'uchidomé'* (play over) sign will light up, and you can no longer use that particular machine.

The catchers, or 'tulips', normally have only a narrow entrance (1). When a ball lands in a catcher, it opens up (2), and if you are lucky, several more balls will land in it before it closes up again (3).

The law limits *'pachinko'* prizes to inexpensive goods, and prohibits cash prizes. When you have finished playing, take any remaining balls to the prize counter and exchange them for your choice of the cigarettes, biscuits and other gifts displayed there.

競輪・競馬をする

BETTING

Gambling is illegal in Japan unless it is sponsored by the Government. However, there is plenty of scope for those who like an occasional flutter, since the Government-backed betting operations cover horse racing, speedboat racing, motorbike racing and bicycle racing (in order of popularity), and public lotteries. A substantial amount of the Government's annual revenue comes from these activities.

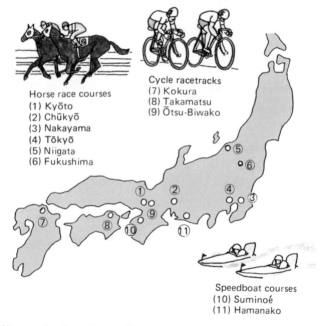

Horse race courses
(1) Kyōto
(2) Chūkyō
(3) Nakayama
(4) Tōkyō
(5) Niigata
(6) Fukushima

Cycle racetracks
(7) Kokura
(8) Takamatsu
(9) Ōtsu-Biwako

Speedboat courses
(10) Suminoé
(11) Hamanako

Horse racing is the biggest form of betting in Japan. There are central race courses in the big cities as well as many local race courses.

88

HOW TO BET ON THE HORSES

1. You can bet on or off track. You can buy one of the many racing papers to help you in your selection.

2. When you have chosen your horse, buy a betting slip.

3. If you are lucky, take your betting slip and collect your winnings.

You can even bet from home if you want to. First, you have to go to a betting office and register; then you can place bets by telephone while watching the races on television. Winnings and losses are sent by bank transfer.

If you don't want to go to the racetrack, you can bet at one of the many off-track betting offices.

In Tōkyō, these are located in Shinjuku, Shibuya, Kōrakuen, Ginza and Kinshichō.

There are many self-appointed experts who predict the winners and sell the information at race courses and betting offices.

武道を習う

STUDYING MARTIAL ARTS

The traditional martial arts of Japan are not practised merely as sports, but are also a means of developing the "samurai spirit". In order to study a martial art, you must enrol at a 'dōjō', or school of martial arts.

Some 'dōjō' are huge, with thousands of pupils, while some local ones have as few as five or six.

There are many different kinds of martial art. Some of the more popular ones are 'jūdō' (judo), 'kendō' (fencing with bamboo swords), 'karaté' (karate), 'aikidō' (similar to judo), 'kyūdō' (Japanese archery) and 'jōdō' (a variation of 'kendō'). Each of these has a number of different schools, or 'ryūha', each with its own philosophical approach and teaching style.

Kendō   Jūdō   Aikidō   Karaté   Kyūdō

When you find a *'dōjō'* that you like the look of, you should ask for permission to observe the training.

If you decide to enrol, you will have to carry out the enrolment formalities and learn the rules of the *'dōjō'*. Other Westerners studying at the *'dōjō'* may be able to help you over any language problems.

Some *'dōjō'* insist that trainees wear the proper costume, so be prepared to spend some money on it.

Since you will be using different muscles and breathing patterns from those you are accustomed to, it's best to take it easy at first.

WATCHING SUMŌ OR BASEBALL

Sumō and baseball are the two most popular sports in Japan. They are reported extensively in newspapers and magazines, and are broadcast on television and radio. However, the only way to appreciate the real excitement and action of these sports is to go to the stadium and see them live.

Six major *'sumō basho'* (tournaments) are held every year, alternately in Tōkyō and elsewhere, according to the following schedule:
January: Tōkyō
March: Ōsaka
May: Tōkyō
July: Nagoya
September: Tōkyō
November: Fukuoka

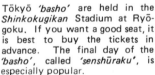

Tōkyō *'basho'* are held in the *Shinkokugikan* Stadium at Ryōgoku. If you want a good seat, it is best to buy the tickets in advance. The final day of the *'basho'*, called *'senshūraku'*, is especially popular.

As well as ordinary seats, there are special boxed areas near the ring known as *'masu'*, each with room for four people. These do not have seats, but are supplied with cushions and an optional meal service. They are the most expensive and give the best view of the *'sumō'*, but those with long legs will find them rather cramped.

Each 'basho' lasts for fifteen days, with wrestling starting in the morning and continuing until about 6 p.m. The lower-ranked wrestlers start first, and the top wrestlers, along with most of the spectators, do not appear until late in the afternoon.

A good way of seeing the top wrestlers close up is to go to the dressing-room and wait for them to come out for the ring-entering ceremony ('dohyōiri'). You cannot go into the dressing-room itself, but you can get a close view.

The wrestlers are divided for the purposes of the tournament into two groups, East and West. Good places to take photographs from are the 'hanamichi', the east and west aisles leading to the 'dohyō' (ring).

The best way of understanding what is happening and who is wrestling is to take a radio (with earphone) with you and listen to the English commentary on FEN (the American Forces' Far East Network).

Baseball is Japan's No.1 sport, and there are games almost every day except in winter. Professional baseball attracts the most attention, with intensive reporting all year round, but the annual All-Japan High-School Baseball Tournament runs a close second.

If you go to see a baseball game, it's best to take a seat on the right or first-base side, since this is where the home team's supporters sit. The visiting team's supporters are on the left, or third-base side.

As well as official supporters' groups, many unofficial fan clubs give vociferous support to their team from the outfield bleachers. The activities of these groups are also fun to watch.

You don't have to leave your seat to get refreshments - just wait for one of the many ice-cream, coca-cola, or beer vendors to come your way. Most of these are students earning a little extra money.

Night games ('naitā') usually start between 6:00 and 6:30 p.m. and last for two or three hours.

Everyone heads for the nearest station as soon as the game is over, and things become pretty crowded; so it is a good plan to buy your ticket when you arrive at the station before the game.

The All-Japan High-School Base-ball Tournament is a knock-out competition held twice a year, in spring and summer, at the Kōshien baseball ground in Hyōgo Pref. It attracts nationwide interest, with everyone fervently supporting their local team, and is loved for its fair play and spirit of amateurism.

ADULT AMUSEMENTS

There are all kinds of ways to amuse oneself in Japan. Here are just a few of them.

Indoor sports such as bowling, ice skating are popular, especially at weekends.

Popularly known as *"Uchippanashi"* (hit & let it lie), there are many driving ranges where you can go to practice golf by yourself. If you don't bring your own clubs, rental is available. Balls are purchased in buckets of about 40, then driven into a fenced-in range with yardage markers. There are also "auto-tennis" practice facilities for tennis buffs and batting cages for would-be pro baseball players.

As well as *'pachinko'* parlours (see p. 86), there are many game centers with TV games of all kinds.

When you are tired out from all these amusements, you can relax in a pub or café bar. These have a cheerful atmosphere and serve beer and other alcoholic drinks as well as coffee, tea, soft drinks and food.

In the evening, many clubs feature live performances by singers and groups. There is standing room only at these clubs when a popular artist is performing.

Discothèques are well patronized by the younger set. They range from smaller, more sophisticated places to huge establishments packed with teenagers. Some have dress codes and some do not admit men unaccompanied by women.

If you have enough money, why not go to a hotel dinner show or a nightclub? These are usually in the American style.

Many of the gaudy neon signs that light up the entertainment districts are advertising strip clubs, "pink cabarets", "peep theaters" and other such esoteric entertainment. Unless you want to be relieved of a lot of money, it's best to visit these places with someone who knows his way around.

The pimps and touts ('*yobikomi*') outside these places clap their hands and try to attract customers. They pay particular attention to passers-by who look as if they have had a bit to drink.

In the back streets of the entertainment districts are many of the well-known "love hotels", identifiable by their purple neon signs. These are for couples only, and some of the bedrooms feature some fairly exotic décor and equipment.

Massage parlours are for men only, and the bath is administered by specially-practised young ladies who offer a range of interesting "services", for a consideration, of course.

ANNUAL EVENTS

The traditional annual events and festivals held in Japan reflect the clear divisions between the four seasons, and often have a religious background. Watching or taking part in them is a good way to get to know Japanese history, culture, and thought a little better.

'*Hatsumōdé*' is the first visit to a temple or shrine in the New Year to pray for health and good luck in the coming year. This is a widely-practised custom, and the better-known shrines and temples are consequently very busy over the New Year holiday period.

Most Japanese visit temples and shrines through custom and tradition rather than for purely religious reasons. Good fortune may be yours, too, if you throw a coin in the collection box *('saisenbako')*, clap your hands, and make a wish.

The third of February each year is the festival of '*setsubun*', the end of winter according to the old calendar. It is the custom on this day to buy roasted soybeans and scatter them around the house to drive out demons, at the same time crying, "*Oni wa soto, fuku wa uchi*"("Out with bad luck, in with good").

Many festivals are associated with the flowers and plants of a particular season. The most popular of these is 'hanami' ("cherry-blossom viewing"), held when the cherry blossoms are at their peak in March or April. 'Hanami' consists of lively drinking parties held under the cherry trees, during the daytime or at night.

There is so much competition for the best 'hanami' spots that some companies send junior employees out in the morning to reserve an area for a party to be held after work that evening.

Just before summer begins, river carnivals known as 'kawabiraki' are held. There is often a fireworks display ('hanabi-taikai'), and many people go to the festival in 'yukata' (cotton 'kimono').

The seventh of July is 'Tanabata', the Star Festival. According to Chinese legend, this is the one night of the year when Altair, the Cowherd, can cross the Milky Way to meet his lover, Vega, the Weaver Princess. Children are taught that their wishes will come true if they write them on decorative strips of paper called 'tanzaku' and hang the strips out on bamboo poles on this day.

As well as the events common to all areas of Japan, thousands of local festivals take place throughout the year, and you are sure to find some near where you are staying or living.

Anyone can take part in the dancing known as *'bon-odori'*. Just join the circle and copy what everyone else is doing, keeping in time with the *'min-yō'* music in the background.

Some festivals feature huge parades and processions. Some of these are modern, with marching bands, trick motorcyclists, and cheer girls, while some are traditional, with the participants dressed in historical costume. A familiar sight at traditional festivals is the *'mikoshi'*, or "portable shrine." These festivals make excellent subjects for camera or video.

The *'Tori-no-ichi'* fair is held each November in the precincts of shrines. At this fair, you can buy good-luck charms such as *'Kumadé'* (a decorative bamboo rake) and *'otafuku'* (a mask of a jolly-looking woman).

At the end of the year, the custom of *'mochitsuki'* (pounding the special rice used for making rice cakes) is held at old people's homes, kindergartens, shrines and other public places. This custom is not as common as it used to be, but it is worth taking part in if you have the chance.

On New Year's Eve (*'Ōmisoka'*), temple bells ring out the old year and ring in the new. This practice is known as *'Joya no kané'*, and, if you are lucky, you might be allowed to ring the bell yourself.

STREET STALLS

A variety of street stalls ('*yatai*') and itinerant vendors can still be seen in Japan, both in the cities and in the country. Some stalls are motorized and some are pushed on foot or by bicycle, and many are equipped with loudspeakers. Each kind of vendor has his own particular cry.

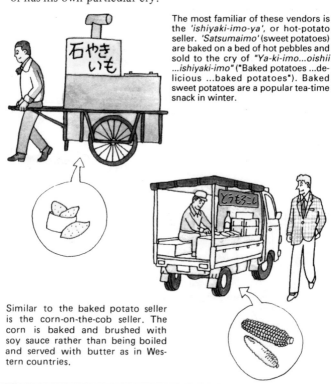

The most familiar of these vendors is the *'ishiyaki-imo-ya'*, or hot-potato seller. *'Satsumaimo'* (sweet potatoes) are baked on a bed of hot pebbles and sold to the cry of *"Ya-ki-imo...oishii ...ishiyaki-imo"* ("Baked potatoes ...delicious ...baked potatoes"). Baked sweet potatoes are a popular tea-time snack in winter.

Similar to the baked potato seller is the corn-on-the-cob seller. The corn is baked and brushed with soy sauce rather than being boiled and served with butter as in Western countries.

Many types of street stall can only be seen in winter. Some of the most popular are as follows:

The 'Oden' stall:
'Oden' is a selection of pressed fish cakes, 'tōfu', hard-boiled eggs, seaweed, Japanese radish ('daikon'), etc., boiled in fish stock. Some vendors move around selling 'oden' only, while some find a good spot near a station or in a busy street and conduct business as a kind of open-air pub, selling beer and 'saké' to go with the 'oden'.

The 'Rāmen' stall:
The 'rāmen' (Chinese noodle) seller is active late at night, when the pubs, clubs, bars, and other drinking-places begin to close, and the drinkers want a light snack before wending their way home.

The 'Tako-yaki' stall:
'Tako-yaki' are a popular snack in the Kansai region, in the west of Japan. They consist of wheat dumplings containing pieces of octopus, cooked on a hot plate while you watch.

Many other dishes, such as 'yakitori' (grilled chicken on a stick), 'isobé-yaki' (baked rice cakes wrapped in seaweed), 'taiyaki' (fish-shaped pancakes filled with sweet bean jam) are sold from street stalls.

Street vendors tour the quieter residential areas as well as busy main streets. The 'tōfu' seller's horn can still be heard in the older parts of the city.

It's best to take some kind of container if you are buying 'tōfu' from a street seller.

Mobile shops selling fresh vegetables, fish, fruit, and other goods often visit 'danchi' (housing complexes) and residential areas which are far from the shops.

Some vendors bring in special deliveries of melons, crabs, or other regional specialities, and tour the city advertising their goods by loudspeaker.

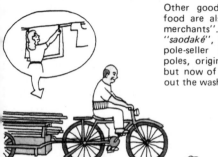

Other goods and services besides food are also offered by "mobile merchants". If you hear the cry "*saodaké*", you will know that the pole-seller is passing by. These poles, originally made of bamboo, but now of plastic, are for hanging out the washing on.

The lively and colorful *'asaichi'*, or "morning markets", are worth visiting if you want to get the freshest fish and vegetables.

Another kind of street stall, seen around stations late at night, is that of the *'ekisha'*, or fortune-teller, who will read your palm or face to divine your future.

釣りぼりへいく

GOING TO FISHING PONDS

In Japan, you can fish in the middle of big cities; not in the rivers, unfortunately, but in man-made, artificially-stocked fishing ponds called *'tsuribori'*. Angling is one of the most popular pastimes in Japan, and the *'tsuribori'* is a good place for busy city-dwellers to steal a few moments of relaxation amid the bustle of city life.

In the sea **In a 'tsuribori'**

It is difficult to find good fishing spots within easy reach of big cities. The *'tsuribori'* is a good substitute — and you are almost certain to catch something.

If you don't have your own bait and tackle, you can hire them at the *'tsuribori'*. Just pay the money in advance.

There are even indoor *'tsuribori'*, called *'hakozuri'*, or "box fishing". These are large pools stocked with smaller varieties of fish.

When you fish at a *'tsuribori'*, you usually have to put back the fish you catch. However, some places will let you take them away with you, and some give out vouchers for each fish caught. These vouchers can be used to defray the cost of your next visit to the *'tsuribori'*, or can be exchanged for prizes of fishing tackle.

TRAVELING IN STYLE

One of the most fascinating aspects of Japan is its combination of the traditional and the modern. However, the only way to appreciate this fully is to get out of the major cities and explore the lesser-known areas.

Whether you like the seaside, the mountains, lakes, rivers, or temples, Japan has any number of beautiful and interesting spots for you to visit. Many of these places are described in pamphlets available in hotels or at railway stations and travel bureaux.

If you are not too confident of your Japanese, it is probably best to let a travel agent handle the transport and accommodation bookings for you.

Once you have learned to speak a little of the language, it is not too difficult to make your own arrangements and travel where the fancy takes you. However, it is advisable to book tickets in advance if you plan to travel by long-distance train in the middle of August or at the end of December, since these are the busiest seasons.

The *'shinkansen'* ("bullet train") is the fastest and most comfortable of Japan's trains. If you take the Tō-kaidō line between Tōkyō and Ōsa-ka, you will have a beautiful view of Mt. Fuji from the landward window.

If you are in too much of a hurry to take the train, you can go by one of Japan's many daily domestic flights. Announcements are made in English both on planes and on the *'shinkansen'*.

Luxury ferry is also a pleasant and relaxing way to travel. Ferries are usually equipped with facilities and amusements to keep passengers from getting bored.

If you hire or buy a car, you can go where you please; but don't forget that, at holiday time, Japan's roads are among the most crowded in the world.

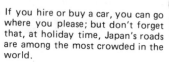

There are many different types of accommodation in Japan; however, the easiest to use are hotels, which are similar to Western hotels and often have English-speaking staff.

The best place in which to stay if you want to experience the traditional lifestyle of Japan is a *'ryokan'*. Breakfast and dinner are included in the price, and the rooms, bath, and service are all in "real Japanese" style.

Many mountain and seaside resorts have small hotels called *'penshon'*, which often have private tennis courts for the use of guests. This type of hotel is usually run by the owner, so you can expect a friendly atmosphere, home cooking and personal service.

Taxi drivers in tourist areas will often act as guides and take you round to see the local sights.

Each area has its own local festivals and events at various times throughout the year. It's a good plan to arrange your travel schedule to include a number of these events.

Another of the great pleasures of traveling is to sample the culinary specialities of the region.

It is customary to buy small souvenirs or gifts of food ('omiyagé') to give to one's friends when one returns from a trip. Your Japanese friends will be delighted if you follow this practice.

TRAVELING ON THE CHEAP

Japan is not a cheap country to travel in, but there are various ways to cut costs.

Some seasons, such as the late summer typhoon season and mid-winter, are not so popular for traveling. However, tickets are cheaper at these times, places are less crowded, and you can experience what it is like in the tourist spots when the weather is not so good.

The rail network in Japan is very extensive. There are more than a thousand different types of discount ticket available, and these can be bought at station travel offices.

Long-distance tickets are proportionately cheaper than short-distance ones, so even if you intend to use a bus or ferry for part of your journey, it may be best to buy the train ticket all the way to your final destination. Excursion tickets are also very handy, since they often cover many different forms of transport.

Traveling overnight on a long distance bus or train can save the cost of a hotel. The Japan Railways runs a coach service between Tōkyō and Ōsaka, and various discount tickets are available which combine this with rail travel.

For sightseeing in cities such as Tōkyō or Kyōto, a day rail pass is recommended. This allows you to make as many journeys as you like within a certain area for as long as the pass is valid.

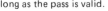

Hitch-hiking is not very common in Japan, but it is easy to get lifts, and people are very helpful. The entrances to motorways are the best places to try, but make sure that you don't break any traffic regulations.

The cheapest places to stay are government guest houses ('*kokumin shukusha*') or youth hostels, if you are a member of the YHA.

Private guest houses, or '*minshuku*' are also cheap and offer a glimpse of Japanese family life. In the cities, "capsule hotels", "business hotels" or the YMCA or YWCA offer low-priced accommodation.

Many temples offer accommodation ('*shukubō*'). It is better to avoid the big ones and approach the smaller ones — you might even be able to pay for some of your bed and board by doing work of some kind.

To cut food costs, you can buy food in shops and make your own picnic, or you can even try cooking for yourself. Especially in the country districts, it is possible to buy fresh vegetables and fish very cheaply at the morning markets.

If the usual restaurants are too expensive, you can save money by eating at the dining halls of libraries, city halls and other public institutions. The variety is limited, but the prices are low.

One of the pleasures of traveling in Japan is to enjoy the many *'ekiben'*, or station lunch boxes. If you are traveling by local train or ordinary express, you can open the window and buy your *'ekiben'* without getting off the train.

TAKING A SIGHTSEEING BUS

An easy way of seeing the sights is to take one of the regular city tour buses, with an English-speaking guide.

There are a number of different routes and programmes, and you can be met and dropped off at most major hotels.

There are half-day tours, full-day tours and night tours, all run on a regular schedule with set days and times.

In big cities such as Tōkyō and Kyōto, tours are arranged to cover most of the better-known sights. Taking one of these tours is a good way to get an overall view of the city before branching off on your own.

A night tour is a good introduction to the night life of Japan, both modern and traditional. Some include an authentic Japanese meal such as a *'sukiyaki'* dinner, some will take you to see a *'kabuki'* play or enjoy a dance party, and some will even introduce you to a *'geisha'* house.

Some special tours introduce you to aspects of Japanese life and culture. These include taking part in a tea ceremony or learning how to put on *'kimono'*.

There is also a tour on which you receive instruction in Japanese cooking, but be careful with this one — you have to eat what you have cooked!

VISITING A HOT SPRING

Japan has more volcanoes and consequently more hot springs ('onsen') than any other country in the world. To the Japanese, the hot spring is a favourite resort.

Many of Japan's hot springs are sulphurous. These can be pretty smelly, and some people do not like them.

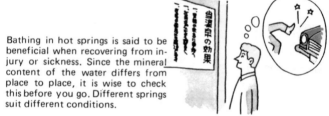

Bathing in hot springs is said to be beneficial when recovering from injury or sickness. Since the mineral content of the water differs from place to place, it is wise to check this before you go. Different springs suit different conditions.

The system for bathing in a hot spring is similar to that for the public bath, but hot springs are usually operated by a *ryokan* (Japanese-style hotel) and are free to the people staying there.

Some people take a dip several times a day, but hot springs can be extremely hot, and it is wise to exercise moderation.

Having a leisurely morning bath (sometimes with a floating tray of 'saké') is one of the most decadently pleasurable things a Japanese can do.

A hot spring is not for getting yourself clean so much as for having a long relaxing soak. Some springs have water so hard that it is impossible to raise a lather from the soap.

Many hot spring resorts are also ski resorts, and a hot dip is sheer bliss after a hard day's skiing.

The best part of a hot spring trip-still hot from the bath, clad in 'yukata' (cotton 'kimono'), drinking 'jizaké' (local 'saké') and sampling the local delicacies, 'sansai' (wild plants) etc.

GOING TO THE SEASIDE

Japan is so long and thin that one is never very far from the sea, and there are many seaside resorts. The most popular season for going to the seaside is from the middle of July, when the rainy season is over, to the middle of August. If you go during this period, be sure to book your accommodation in advance.

Vital items for the beach

Most of these items can be rented at the beach - but the rental fees are not cheap.

Beach parasol

Swim ring

Groundsheet

Folding chair

Beach sandals

'Kakigōri' (shaved ice)

'Yakisoba' (fried noodles)

Hot dogs

During the season, temporary beach cafés ply a busy trade. Many of these have cubicles with showers for hire. These are handy when you are on a day trip and are not staying in the area.

The food served at beach cafés is usually quite expensive, so it's better to bring your own picnic.

Surfing is very popular among young people in Japan. When you take a dip, mind you don't get hit by a surfboard.

Some beaches have a designated safety area marked off by strings of white floats. The lifeguards make sure that all swimmers stay in this area.

There are plenty of *'ryokan'* (Japanese-style hotels) and cheaper *'minshuku'* (guest houses) at seaside resorts. Good guests make sure they wash off all the sand at the shower outside before entering their hotel.

Fireworks are popular at the seaside in summer, and so is *'suika-wari'*, a game in which people are blindfolded and try to break open a watermelon with a stick. Of course, the watermelon is eaten afterwards.

PROVERBS

Proverbs are often quoted in Japan when giving advice or pointing a moral. Some of the more commonly-heard ones are given below:

♦ *Gō ni ittewa gō ni shitagaé*

"When in Rome, do as the Romans do"; i.e., when you are in a foreign country, try to follow the manners and customs of the people of that country.

♦ *Kōbō mo fudé no ayamari*

"Even Homer sometimes nods"; i.e., even the best of us can make mistakes. This sentiment is also expressed by the proverb "*saru mo ki kara ochiru*" (even a monkey sometimes falls from his tree).

♦ *Hyakubun wa ikken ni shikazu*

"Seeing is believing", or "A single picture is worth a thousand words".

♦ *Nakittsura ni hachi*
"Misfortunes never come singly"; i.e., if you have one piece of bad luck, you can always expect another.

UNDERSTANDING

ATTENDING A WEDDING

Weddings, like funerals, are rather traditional affairs in Japan, so if you are invited to one, it's best to know some of the etiquette before you go.

If you cannot attend, the happy couple will appreciate a telegram. You can send these over the telephone (dial 115) or you can go to the post office and fill in a form.

When you receive the invitation, quickly return the enclosed post-card, indicating whether you can attend or not. In either case, you should write a few words of con-gratulation on the card.

Standard dress for weddings

Black bow tie or white or silver necktie

Dinner jacket or *'reifuku'* (black formal suit — can be bought or hired)

Dress - any colour except white (only the bride wears white)

Black shoes

Weddings in Japan can be *Shintō*, Buddhist or Christian, and the style chosen does not have to depend on the couple's religion.

If the wedding is a *Shintō* one, usually only the couple's close family attend the actual ceremony. If you are lucky enough to be invited to join them, just watch carefully and copy what everybody else does.

Wedding presents are not usually given in Japan; instead, the guests bring cash. This should be placed in a special envelope called *'shūgi-bukuro'*, available at stationers and station kiosks, and handed in at the reception. Consult a Japanese friend to help you decide how much to give.

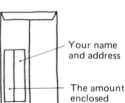

Outside

御結婚御祝

Your name

Inside

Your name and address

The amount enclosed

At the reception, the *'nakōdo'* (matchmaker) first makes a speech, and then the main guests make speeches. During this, everybody listens quietly, without touching the food or drink.

Next, a toast is proposed, and then the guests are free to eat, drink and talk. After a while, the *'shikaisha'* (master of ceremonies) starts to ask various friends of the bride or groom to make speeches or sing songs. It is all right to go on eating and drinking during this, but you should not talk in a loud voice.

The following words should be avoided in speeches at weddings: *'kireru'* (to be cut or broken), *'hanareru'* (to separate) and *'wakareru'* (to separate). All these words imply divorce.

Smoking during important ceremonies is considered bad manners, so it's best not to smoke during the reception.

If you have to leave the room to go to the toilet or telephone, wait until no speeches are being made or the bride and groom have retired to change their clothes, excuse yourself to the guests on either side of you and leave the room quietly.

After the reception, guests take their leave of the newly-wedded couple at the door. Each guest receives a present, called 'hikidé-mono'.

Many young couples these days forego a formal reception in favour of a more relaxed, party-type gathering.

ATTENDING A FUNERAL

The Japanese do not seem to be particularly concerned with religion in their daily lives, but they are sticklers for tradition when it comes to funerals. You'll be missing out on an important aspect of Japanese life if you don't familiarize yourself with the etiquette used on such occasions.

Men should wear a black necktie.

The dress worn by mourners attending a funeral should be basically black.

The only jewellery acceptable for women to wear is pearls.

The handbag should also be black. Many mourners carry a Buddhist rosary ('*juzu*').

The suit should be black, dark grey or dark blue.

kōden-bukuro

Write your name here.

Put the condolence money ('*kōden*') in this special envelope ('*kōden-bukuro*') available from stationers or station newsstands.

When you get near the house where the funeral is being held, look out for the directions posted on the telephone poles.

Mourners attending a funeral take with them a gift of money for the bereaved family, as an expression of condolence. How much to give is rather a delicate question, so it is best to discuss this with a Japanese friend before you go.

On arriving at the entrance, you should bow once, then hand over your condolence money in its envelope and write your name and address in the book provided. This is so that the bereaved family can write and thank everybody who attended the funeral, so make sure that you write your address correctly.

Paying one's respects to the deceased.

1. Bow once to the bereaved family.

2. Briefly contemplate the memorial tablet ('*ihai*') and the picture of the late departed ('*iei*').

3. Place the hands together and pray, then lower the hands to the knees.

Offering incense:

1. With the right hand, take a pinch of incense from the incense casket.

2. Raise the right hand holding the incense level with the forehead.

3. Place the incense in the incense burner, then repeat steps 1 to 3 twice more.

4. Place the hands together in prayer once more, then bow again to the bereaved family once, and leave.

Most funerals last for two days. The evening and night of the first day are called 'tsuya' (wake, or vigil), while the ceremony that takes place during the second day is called 'kokubetsushiki' (leave-taking). Mourners call on one of the two days, depending on which one best fits in with their schedule.

Guests attending the 'tsuya' may be invited into a separate room for refreshments after they have offered incense.

Close friends and relatives will accept the invitation and gather to exchange thoughts about the deceased. However, it is usual to decline the invitation unless you are a very close friend of the family.

When eventually leaving, guests who have stayed for the refreshments offer incense once again and say a few words of condolence ('o-kuyami') to the family of the deceased before making their way home.

Guests attending the *'kokubetsu-shiki'* will first offer incense and then wait outside the house for the coffin to be brought out and placed in the hearse (*'reikyūsha'*). This "leave-taking ceremony" is over very quickly, so it is important to get to the house by the appointed time, or you will miss the ceremony entirely.

The hearse then departs with the body for the crematorium. In Japan, all bodies must be cremated, and the law does not allow burial.

Everyone attending a funeral is given a small packet of salt which he should have sprinkled on him before entering his house. Salt has been used since olden times in Japan in sacred purification rites, and this particular ceremony is to remove any traces of other-worldly influences that may remain about the person of someone who has attended a funeral.

EXCHANGING GIFTS

Gifts help to create good relations among people in Japan just as in other countries. The big gift-giving seasons in Japan are *'chūgen'*, in July, and *'seibo'*, in December. Some people give each other Christmas and birthday presents, but this is not as common as it is in Western countries.

During *'chūgen'* and *'seibo'*, department stores put gift packs on sale and set up special departments to take the orders and send out the gifts. Popular items include wine and whisky; fruit, ham, canned goods, soap, and cooking oil.

To send one of these gifts, all you have to do is to fill in a form with your name and address and the recipient's name and address, and pay the money. The department store will take care of the rest.

Having the gift sent is usually quite acceptable, but it is considered good manners to deliver a gift personally if it is to a very close acquaintance, especially one who has done you a great favour.
The Japanese usually send *'chūgen'* and *'seibo'* to their former teachers or university professors, and to their *'nakōdo'* (matchmaker) if appropriate.

If you receive a present at *'chūgen'* or *'seibo'*, it is not necessary to give anything in return. However, do not omit to send a letter of thanks.

If you receive a present on another occasion, such as your wedding, the birth of a child, an illness, or the death of a family member, you should give in return a gift worth about half the value of the one you received. This custom is called *'hangaeshi'*.

At New Year, children usually receive pocket money, called *'otoshidama'*, from relatives and friends of the family. You will create a good impression if you follow this custom and give some to your friends' children. Place the money in the special envelope called *'otoshidamabukuro'* available from stationers'.

GOOD AND BAD LUCK

Superstition is a natural part of Japanese life and thought, but young people nowadays ignore or are unaware of many of the old beliefs.

The north-east is considered unlucky, since it is the direction by which demons enter and leave. It even has a special name('*kimon*'), which means "devils' gate", and it is bad to build a house with the entrance facing this way.

It is also thought unlucky to sleep with the head towards the north '*kitamakura*', since this is how dead bodies are laid out.

Certain days are either lucky or unlucky, and are noted on calendars. The most important ones are '*Tai-an*', a lucky day which is excellent for weddings, and '*Butsumetsu*', which is unlucky but good for funerals. Wedding halls are virtually empty on '*Butsumetsu*' days in spite of the special low prices they offer as an inducement.

The number four is unlucky, since one of its pronunciations, *'shi'*, can also mean "death". Hospital rooms are always numbered 1, 2, 3, 5, ...

Japanese children sometimes make a paper doll called *'teru-terubōzu'* and hang it outside the window to bring fine weather the next day.

'Ashita tenki ni nāré'

It's a lucky sign to find a stalk floating upright in your teacup. This event is described by the phrase *'chabashira ga tatsu'*.

ZAZEN

'Zazen' is widely practised in Japan, not only by *'zen'* believers, but also by ordinary people as a form of spiritual training. It is well worth trying if you have the chance.

'Zen' temples hold regular *'zazen'* sessions. These are usually open to everybody, and foreign tourists or residents are welcome.

HOW TO SIT

The basic position is the "full lotus" position (*'kekka fuza'*).
1. Place the right foot on the left thigh.
2. Place the left foot on the right thigh.

If this is too difficult,
1. Press the right foot against the inside of the left thigh.
2. Place the left foot on top of the right foot with one ankle on top of the other.

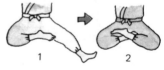

1   2   1   2

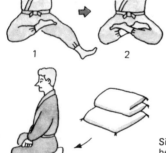

Sitting on two cushions like this will help to relieve the pain usually experienced when first trying *'zazen'*.

There are many different hand positions.

Keep the upper body straight and the shoulders relaxed.

(1)   (2)   (3)

BREATHING

The most important thing in *'zazen'* is to breathe in plenty of good fresh air and thereby induce a state of deep meditation. The easiest method of breathing is the *'shōshūten'* method described below.

1. With the eyes half-closed (*'hangan'*) draw in the breath and feel it moving from the base of the spine up the backbone and over the top of the head, coming to rest at the ponit midway between the eyes (*'miken'*).
2. Hold the breath and imagine a powerful source of light and warmth, like the sun, radiating from the *'miken'*.
3. Release the breath and feel it flowing down over the center of the face, throat and chest to the abdomen about an inch below the navel (*'tanden'*).
4. Repeat.

EASTERN MEDICINE

Eastern medicine, with its thousands of years of tradition, is widely practised in Japan along with modern Western medicine. The Eastern medicine practised in Japan originated mainly in China. It is designed to stimulate the natural healing powers of the body, and it rarely produces any of the undesirable side-effects sometimes associated with Western medicine.

One of the most popular forms of Eastern medicine is *'hari'*, or acupuncture. The acupuncturist stimulates certain points on the body, called *'tsubo'*, by inserting thin silver needles. This procedure does not hurt, and the healing effects can be dramatic.

The needles used in acupuncture are hair-thin. The *'tsubo'* into which they are inserted are said to be connected to particular internal organs, and the acupuncturist will select the *'tsubo'* to match the symptoms of the patient. There are more than three hundred *'tsubo'* on the human body.

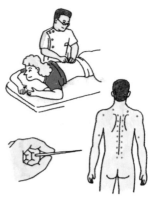

Another form of medicine associated with acupuncture is *'okyū'*, or moxibustion. In moxibustion, the *'tsubo'* are stimulated by burning small amounts of *'mogusa'* (moxa, a powder made from dried leaves) on the skin over the *'tsubo'*.

There are many other ways of stimulating the *'tsubo'* and thus increasing the activity of the associated internal organs. One of these is *'shiatsu'*, or finger-pressure therapy.

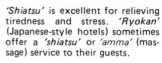

'Shiatsu' is excellent for relieving tiredness and stress. *'Ryokan'* (Japanese-style hotels) sometimes offer a *'shiatsu'* or *'amma'* (massage) service to their guests.

Most Japanese know the locations of some of the *'tsubo'* even though they may not have studied *'shiatsu'* formally. It is quite common for family members or friends to massage or pound each other's shoulders, a simple form of *'shiatsu'* called *'katatataki'*.

If you suffer a dislocation or sprain, you can visit a *'sekkotsu-shi'*, or "bone-setter". Most *jūdō* teachers are trained in this technique.

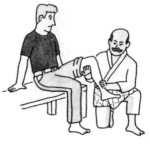

For stomach upsets or other ailments, you might like to try *'kampōyaku'* (Chinese herbal medicine), since it is said to have no side-effects. It can be bought at most pharmacists'.

Place a length of split bamboo on the floor and tread on it for a few minutes every day. This stimulates the *'tsubo'* on the soles of the feet and relieves tiredness. This treatment is called *'aotake-fumi'*.

The same effect is achieved by having someone stand on your feet or walk up and down your back.

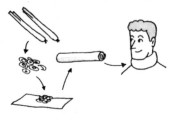

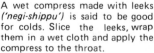

A wet compress made with leeks *('negi-shippu')* is said to be good for colds. Slice the leeks, wrap them in a wet cloth and apply the compress to the throat.

To cure a headache, take the stones out of a pair of *'umeboshi'* (salted plums) and apply the plums to the temples.

Standing on the head stimulates the *'tsubo'* on the top of the head and is therefore very good for the health.

A ginger poultice *('shōga-shippu')* is good for a number of complaints. To make one, follow the steps shown in the picture:

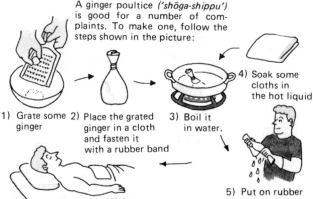

1) Grate some ginger

2) Place the grated ginger in a cloth and fasten it with a rubber band

3) Boil it in water.

4) Soak some cloths in the hot liquid

5) Put on rubber gloves and wring out the cloths

6) Place the cloths on the affected part. This treatment is excellent for stomachache.

143

SOROBAN AND CALCULATOR

The *'soroban'*, or abacus, is still a very popular calculating aid in Japan, and is used in many shops.

The top row of beads represents 5s, 50s, 500s,etc., in order from right to left, while the bottom rows represent 1s, 10s, 100s, etc. The *'soroban'* is cleared to zero by raising all the top beads and lowering all the bottom beads, away from the central bar. Addition, subtraction, multiplication and division are then performed by flicking the appropriate beads towards or away from the central bar.

The Japanese are generally good at mental arithmetic (*'anzan'*), but those proficient at the *'soroban'* are particularly quick, since they can picture a *'soroban'* in their heads while calculating.

Many people, especially businessmen, prefer to use electronic calculators *('dentaku')* these days, since they can be used with hardly any practice.

There are all kinds of electronic calculator, some the size and thickness of a visiting card, and some built into pens, lighters and wristwatches. There is even a combined *'soroban'* and calculator on the market.

For simple calculations, the *'soroban'* is just as fast as the calculator. The *'soroban'* is popular as an extra-curricular subject to help children who are not very good at arithmetic.

CRIME

Japanese newspapers are full of reports of big "Western-style" crimes and juvenile delinquency, but on the whole, Japan is still a safe, law-abiding country.

The crime rate in Japan is about a fifth of that in America and Europe, and the criminal is arrested in about sixty percent of cases.

1994 White Paper on Crime: Arrests as percentage of total criminal offences: 58.1%

It is quite safe to take the subway late at night. Mugging is almost unheard of, but it is wise to take precautions against pickpockets. Women, especially foreign women, should also beware of the notorious *'chikan'*, whose activities include taking advantage of the crowded trains to put their hands where they shouldn't be, exposing themselves to women returning home through quiet back streets late at night, stealing women's underwear, etc.

You will get into serious trouble in Japan for any of the activities shown here, which are all criminal offences.

Using or being in possession of marijuana or other drugs.

Driving while under the influence of alcohol.

PROHIBIT!

Being in possession of pornographic materials.

Being in possession of firearms.

BUSINESS

Before trying to do business in Japan, it is vital to have some understanding of the way Japanese society works and of the Japanese way of doing business.

Always make an appointment by telephone before you visit a company to talk to someone on business. Many company employees take their lunch break between twelve and one.

When people meet for the first time, business cards ('*meishi*') are always exchanged before discussion starts. '*Meishi*' are indispensable to anyone living or working in Japan.

Keep your '*meishi*' in an inside front pocket. It is bad manners to offer someone a '*meishi*' that has been kept in the back pocket of your trousers.
It is also inadvisable to jot notes on another person's '*meishi*'. Some people consider this rude.

In Japanese companies, decisions are rarely based on individual responsibility. People either rely on the consensus of the group, or follow the directions of a senior manager. Expect business discussions to take time to bear fruit, since many people are included in the decision-making.

Formal meetings in Japan are usually held after the decisions have been made. They are not for the purpose of reaching decisions, but to announce the decisions that have already been reached by the process known as *'nemawashi'. 'Nemawashi'*, or "root-binding", is a horticultural term which in business parlance means the reaching of a consensus prior to its formal ratification.

This consensus is reached through informal discussions and the circulation of a document known as the *'ringi'*, on which all the relevant people put their seal of approval.

Two terms people often use when talking about Japanese companies are *'nenkō-joretsu-sei'* (the seniority system) and *'shūshin-koyō-sei'* (the lifetime employment system). In the first, employees are promoted by seniority rather than by ability, and in the second, employees have a safe job for life provided they do not make any massive blunders.

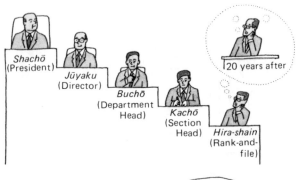

Shachō
(President)

Jūyaku
(Director)

Buchō
(Department Head)

20 years after

Kachō
(Section Head)

Hira-shain
(Rank-and-file)

Employees who are loyal to their companies work more as a team than as a collection of individuals. When introducing themselves, they often give their company name before their own, and refer to each other by their positions within the company; e.g., by *'kachō'* (section head) rather than by their names.

New staff are often chosen through the *'ōbī'* ("old boy") network or through other types of *'koné'* (connection).

Here are some tips for non-Japanese employees of Japanese companies:

1. Be prepared to spend time socializing with your colleagues after working hours.

2. A confident manner is appropriate, but you will meet with resistance if you try to be too pushy.

1,000,000 dollars

? yen

3. Converting figures, dates and other detailed information between Japanese and English is not easy even for those who speak both languages well. Always check such information carefully, writing it down if possible.

Business and working relationships in Japan depend far more on trust than on written contracts. If you want your work in Japan to go smoothly, you will have to show people that you are reliable, honest and trustworthy.

THE JAPANESE FACTORY

One of the secrets of Japan's economic success is the high productivity of its factories. These are built on spacious sites on the outskirts of cities, and are run very efficiently.

Employees usually attend a morning assembly *('chōrei')* before they start work. At the assembly, they do physical exercises, listen to a pep talk, or discuss the day's goals.

Each worker knows his own responsibility and is very conscious of the importance of his role in the group.

Everyday problems are solved through discussion and analysis carried out by quality control circles.

Regular sports days, events and company outings are held for employees and their families to strengthen their team spirit.

Employees work hard and conscientiously, and earn their lunch break, which they spend playing sports, dozing, or playing games such as *'igo'* (go) or *'shōgi'* (Japanese chess).

There is usually a tea break at about 3 p.m., and many groups tune in to the physical exercise programme on the radio (*'rajio taisō'*) and have another short workout.

GOING TO PARTIES

Parties are regarded by the Japanese as a good way of relaxing their normally rather formal relationships, letting their hair down a bit, and getting to know each other better. However, unlike in the West, parties are rarely held in private homes; they are more often held by organized groups such as town associations, societies, and groups of business colleagues or school and university classmates, than by groups of personal friends.

Most Japanese like drinking socially and need little excuse to get together and knock a few back. The big party season is at the end of December, when *'bōnenkai'* (literally, "forget-the-year-parties") are held to see out the old year, and at the beginning of January, when *'shinnenkai'* (New Year's parties) are held to welcome in the new. Weddings and funerals are both legitimate occasions for getting together and drinking, as is the cherry blossom season in spring, when *'hanami'* ("flower viewing") parties are held under the cherry trees.

A *'kanji'* (master of ceremonies, or party organizer) is always chosen to be in charge of the arrangements.

The *'kanji'* draws up the guest list, arranges the venue, handles the money, keeps everyone informed, and presides over the party itself.

Seats are not usually allocated except at formal dinners, but if the party is held in a Japanese room, the more important guests should be seated in the 'kamiza' area, in front of the 'tokonoma' (alcove, see p. 20). The more important the guest, the nearer he should be to the 'kamiza' area, while the least important guests must be content with the 'shimoza' area near the door.

Most parties are held in restaurants or special banquet halls, rarely in offices or homes.

When people have had a bit to drink, the entertainment begins, and the guests show their hidden talent ('kakushigei') for singing, dancing, mime, etc.

You may be invited to visit a Japanese home, but don't bring your family unless you are asked to. Japanese houses are small compared to Western ones, and there isn't room for a lot of guests.

Spouses are not usually invited to office parties, and people rarely invite their business colleagues to their homes.

However, wives often get together in the daytime when their husbands are at work.

Children have birthday parties with presents and a cake with candles, just like in the West.

Young people living alone sometimes invite their friends to a party, but they are usually rather quiet affairs. There is no room for dancing, and the walls are so thin that the neighbours soon complain if the music is too loud. If you are invited to one of these, don't forget to take along some food and drink.

Student clubs and societies regularly hold cheap, rowdy drinking parties called *'konpa'* at which the cry of *"ikki! ikki!"* ("down in one!") is often heard. Groups of the opposite sex also gather for *'gōkon'* (mixed drinking sessions) to give men students and women students an opportunity to meet each other.

Former schoolmates sometimes hold parties *('dōsōkai')* at which they reminisce about their childhood days.

Relatives who do not usually meet will often gather for *'hōji'*, a Buddhist memorial service, usually held on the first, second, seventh and thirteenth anniversary of a person's death. Naturally, there is a party with food and drink after the service.

日本の家族

A TYPICAL JAPANESE FAMILY

Most Japanese families these days consist of two parents and one or two children *('kakukazoku')*. Modern homes, especially in the cities, suffer from lack of space, and it is becoming less and less usual for married couples to live together with their parents, even though most of them would like to.

The goal of most married couples is to have their own house, but this is a costly business in Japan. Many young couples cannot afford it, and live in rented accommodation or subsidised company housing *('shataku')*.

THE AVERAGE FAMILY
1988~1989 Statistics:

Percentage of families having 4 members:	24%
Home ownership ratio:	61.3%
Average commuting time:	47.4 min.
Average savings:	¥9,950,000
Percentage of households having three generations living together:	15%
Percentage of homes with separate room(s) for children:	76%
Percentage of people who regard themselves as middle-class:	88.5%
Average monthly pocket money for primary-school children:	¥2,814

Most Japanese children start their education at a nursery (0 – 5 yrs old) or kindergarten (3–5 yrs), although this is not compulsory.

Primary school is for six years, from the age of six to the age of twelve. There are three school terms a year, and the school year starts in April. Holidays are taken in summer and at New Year. The children are given an oppressively heavy load of homework.

After lessons, most primary-school children have extracurricular lessons in activities such as swimming, *'soroban'* (abacus) or piano. Their daily schedule is harder than that of most adults.

After primary school, all children complete three years of junior high school. They start to learn English at junior high school, but since not many teachers can speak English or understand it when it is spoken, the children study mainly grammar, and make little progress on the conversational side.

Although it is not compulsory, 94% of junior-high-school pupils go on to complete three years of high school, and a large proportion of these then do a four-year college course. There is tremendous competition to get into the prestige universities such as the University of Tōkyō, and high-school students are subjected to the intense pressure of the *'juken jigoku'*, or "examination hell".

Some high-school students who fail to get into the university of their choice do a further year's study at a *'yobikō'*, or cramming school, before taking the university entrance exam again. These students are called *'rōnin'*.

Japanese universities are hard to get into and easy to graduate from. Almost all students take a part-time job, not to support themselves, but to earn pocket money.

More and more women are working these days, but almost all of them stop working when they get married or have children. They are called *'sengyō shufu'*, or full-time housewives.

Average age at which Japanese get married:

Men: 28.5
Women: 26.2

In most households, the wife does all the housework, without the help of a maid.

Even when both husband and wife are working, the wife tends to do the greater part of the housework, although many young couples try to apportion the household chores equally. Society is not set up for the working mother, and facilities such as day nurseries are hard to find.

Most companies pay their employees monthly. The wife usually looks after the family finances and gives the husband a certain sum of pocket money each month —but both husband and wife often have some secret savings, called 'hesokuri', for their private use.

Businessmen often work late or go out drinking with their colleagues after work, so it is a rare event for a man to have dinner with his family on weekdays.

A man will see his family even less often if his company sends him to work in another city, since he will probably go unaccompanied. This is so as to avoid interrupting the children's schooling with unsettling moves. Some married men work abroad for years and only see their family occasionally.

Husbands and wives rarely express their feelings for each other openly in words such as "I love you", and a bow is far more usual than a kiss when hubby leaves for work in the morning or comes home at night.

The wife usually calls her husband *'anata'*, while the husband calls his wife by her name or by the term *'oi'* ("Hey you!"). Couples with children may call each other *'otōsan'* (Daddy) and *'okāsan'* (Mummy).

The Japanese are sometimes very disparaging when talking about their own family members. This is often because, although secretly very proud, they do not want to appear boastful or conceited.

Mothers whose children have grown up often attend cultural centers to study or pursue hobbies. They are also fond of sports such as tennis, aerobics, and golf.

Time to look for another job.

The retiring age (*'teinen'*) for most people is fifty-five or sixty. Even though they receive a pension (*'nenkin'*), many people find another job and continue working, either for economic reasons or because they do not know how to settle down to a life of leisure.

One of the most popular pastimes for senior citizens these days is "gateball", a game resembling croquet.

Many families consider that the eldest son, who is also the main heir, should continue to live with them even after he is married. Quarrels between the son's wife (*'yomé'*) and her mother-in-law (*'shūtomé'*) are not unusual.

Even if they are not actually living together, married couples spend a lot of time with their parents, and usually try to meet at least twice a year, for *'obon'* in summer and again at New Year.

Although Japanese houses are usually too small to permit children, parents and grandparents to live together, most families like, if possible, to have the grandparents living close by.

SOME GEOGRAPHICAL FACTS

Japan is a mountainous country with many volcanoes. The highest mountain in Japan is Mt. Fuji (*Fujisan*), at 3776 m. The longest river is the River Shinano (*Shinanogawa*), which flows through Nagano and Niigata Prefectures. Its length of 367 km is one-twentieth of that of the Nile.

Japan's largest lake is the 673.8 km² Lake Biwa, in Shiga Prefecture.

The highest temperature ever recorded in Japan was 40.8°C, in the city of Yamagata, on the 25th of July, 1933, while the lowest was −41.0°C in Asahikawa, Hokkaidō, on 25th of January, 1902.

[APPENDIX]

SELF-EXPRESSION

In dealing with other people, the Japanese tend to play down their own feelings and opinions, preferring to concentrate on creating harmonious, confrontation-free relationships. They express their feelings indirectly so as to avoid shocking other people or making them feel uncomfortable.

The Japanese smile: Happiness or welcome is usually expressed in a restrained fashion, with the mouth and eyes alone, rather than with the whole body.

Hi, Mr. Satō! That was a pretty girl I saw you with last night!

It is easy to be misled by the Japanese smile, because, as well as expressing happiness or amusement, it is also often used to cover confusion or embarrassment.

Anger: The Japanese rarely express anger openly or lose their temper, especially in public, even when they disagree with someone. They will often apologize to an angry person to calm him down, even when they believe themselves to be in the right.

Losing one's temper is considered childish, so when most Japanese feel anger, they automatically try to suppress it.

When two people fall out over something, they make every effort to settle the dispute amicably, through such means as discussion or going out for a drink together.

Sadness: While bad at expressing anger, the Japanese have many subtle ways of expressing sadness.

To be considered adult in Japanese society, a person must be able to hide pain or sorrow behind a smile. This is called *'kao de waratte kokoro de naku'* (a smile on the face and tears in the heart).

Although men are expected to control their emotions and hide sadness, it is occasionally all right for a man to cry. This is called *'otokonaki'*, and it shows that a man is not, after all, as cold and unemotional as he might appear.

'Morainaki' means "crying in sympathy", and it is permissible to indulge in it freely, since it shows human feeling rather than weakness.

If you see a Japanese in floods of tears, it does not necessarily mean that he or she is sad. It can be a sign of great happiness, as when one's home team has won at baseball. This form of tears is called *'ureshinaki'* ("happy crying").

Being shy is not looked down on as a sign of immaturity in Japan, but is regarded as an attractive quality, especially when it concerns romantic feelings.

To express one's wishes openly is considered at best naive, and at worst, rude. This is because it may not be convenient for the other person to accommodate your wishes, in which case you have put him in the embarrassing position of having to refuse.

The Japanese are very sensitive to subtle gestures and other forms of non-verbal communication.

Many Japanese believe that, if they have to use words to communicate their feelings, then they are not truly communicating. They would prefer to have the other person understand what they want through intuition, rather than express their feelings verbally.

The Japanese system of non-verbal communication is an efficient way of communicating emotions but is unsuitable for complex matters involving rational discussion.

The Japanese hate saying no directly. They prefer to use expressions such as *"kangaeté mimasu"* ("I'll think about it"), *"zensho shimasu"* ("I'll see what I can do about it."), or *"sā...sore wa chotto muzukashii"* ("Well, I'm afraid that would be a little difficult"). This is done to avoid creating an unpleasant atmosphere, but Westerners who prefer to call a spade a spade often find it annoying.

Some Japanese easily fall into the role of listener, nodding and saying "Yes, yes", rather than expressing their own opinions positively. This can mislead the speaker into believing that his listener is agreeing with him, when in fact the opposite may be true.

In order to get on well in Japan, you will have to try continually to create harmonious relationships, avoid disputes, and make an effort to understand the way people express their emotions. Remember that, behind their "inscrutable smiles", the Japanese are as human as the rest of us.

PHYSIQUE

Japan is an island country, and different areas are culturally very similar. There are also a number of physical characteristics common to all Japanese.

The most obvious distinguishing characteristic of the Japanese is their black or dark-brown hair and eyes.

The Japanese tend to be taller than other Asians, their average height being about the same as that of the French.

The average Japanese has a longer body and shorter legs than the average American or European. This is thought to be because of the Japanese diet, which is based on rice and includes a lot of vegetables and not much meat.

Perhaps because of their physique, the Japanese are good at sports such as judo, wrestling, gymnastics and weightlifting, all of which require a low center of gravity.

Many Japanese put on weight as they get older, just like people in other countries. The need to take exercise has become more and more widely recognized, and many people are taking up jogging and other sports.

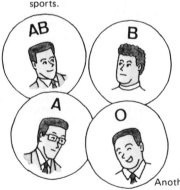

Another aspect of physique is blood type. Many young people believe that one's character is determined by one's blood type, and most people can soon tell you whether they are A, B, O, or AB.

BODY LANGUAGE

Scratching the head is a way of hiding confusion or embarrassment.

Holding up the index fingers like horns on either side of the forehead indicates that a third person (perhaps a boss or wife) is angry.

Holding a clenched fist beside the head and suddenly opening the fingers expresses the opinion that a person is 'pā' (stupid or crazy).

Folding the arms shows that a person is thinking hard.

Holding a clenched fist in front of the face in imitation of a long nose implies that the person under discussion is, like the long-nosed goblin *'Tengu'*, a conceited braggart.

Touching the index fingers together like swords clashing indicates that people are quarrelling.

The gesture of applying saliva to the eyebrow shows that you are not taken in by the tall story your friend is telling you.

When passing in front of people, excuse yourself by stooping slightly and holding out the hand with the edge downwards as if you are cutting your way through.

ETIQUETTE

マナー集

A knowledge of the manners and etiquette of a country can give much insight into that country's social system and ways of thinking. It can also help you to avoid social gaffes. Some basic Japanese table manners are introduced here.

If you eat Japanese food, you will of course have to use 'hashi' (chopsticks). These should be placed on the table pointing to the diner's left, with the tips resting on the 'hashioki' (chopstick rest). Take the chopsticks in your right hand and transfer them to the left hand. Then take the proper grip on them with the fingers of the right hand.

The following actions are considered bad manners:

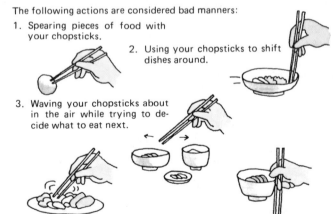

1. Spearing pieces of food with your chopsticks.

2. Using your chopsticks to shift dishes around.

3. Waving your chopsticks about in the air while trying to decide what to eat next.

4. Rummaging about in the food looking for the tastiest morsel.

5. Picking up a dish with the hand that is holding the chopsticks.

Westerners taught not to make a noise when eating soup are often surprised to find that, in Japan, it is all right to slurp one's noodles.

Don't start eating the soup as soon as it is placed in front of you. Japanese meals are usually served all at once, rather than as separate courses, so you should wait until all the food is on the table and everyone is ready before you begin.

Place your chopsticks on your 'hashioki' when you are not using them. If you plant them vertically in your rice, you will give your table companions a shock, as this is how rice is offered by Buddhists to their deceased ancestors.

Itadakimasu !

Before starting a meal, say 'Itadakimasu'; after finishing, say 'Gochisōsama'.

There are many rules of etiquette for the use of Japanese-style rooms ('*washitsu*'). Here are two of the simpler ones:

Do not step on the doorsill or the borders of the '*tatami*' mats.

When a person wears '*kimono*', he or she is expected to observe a certain standard of deportment. People wearing '*kimono*' should not leap about or indulge in exaggerated gestures, but should allow the '*kimono*' to impart a natural grace to their actions.

The correct way of opening or closing a '*fusuma*' or '*shōji*' (sliding paper door) is to kneel on the floor, grasp the door below its center with both hands, and slide it quietly open or shut. However, this is only done on formal occasions nowadays.

When visiting someone in hospital, it is good manners to take the invalid a present. Some easily-digestible food such as fruit is probably best. Cut flowers are acceptable, but pot plants should be avoided, as these are thought to cause illnesses to take a firmer root.

SOME OTHER POINTS OF ETIQUETTE

If you move house, it is customary to introduce yourself to your new neighbors, taking along a small gift such as soap or hand towels.

It is usual to dress smartly at weddings or other parties, even if the invitation says "come as you are".

The Japanese send New Year's cards ('nengajō') to their friends and relations. However, cards are not sent to anyone who has had a death in the family during the previous year.

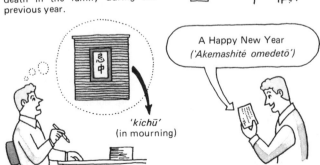

'kichū'
(in mourning)

A Happy New Year
('Akemashité omedetō')

FAUX PAS OFTEN MADE BY JAPANESE WHEN DEALING WITH FOREIGNERS:

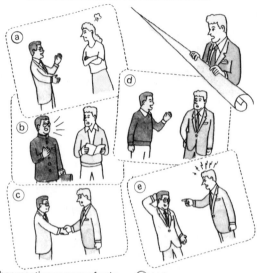

(a) When meeting someone for the first time, asking personal questions such as a man's salary, or age, marital status, or apartment rent.

(b) Confusing someone's first name with their surname.

(c) Holding the hand out limply, like a wet fish, when shaking hands, and then forgetting to let go at the appropriate time. The handshake is a relatively new custom in Japan, and many people are not yet used to it.

(d) Using a person as a target for English conversation practice.

(e) Grinning and bowing when apologizing. This is done to hide embarrassment, but it can give the impression that the apologizer is not taking the matter seriously and is not sincere in what he is saying.

FAUX PAS OFTEN MADE BY FOREIGNERS WHEN DEALING WITH JAPANESE:

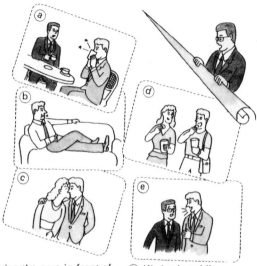

(a) Blowing the nose in front of people. If you want to blow your nose, you should leave your seat or turn away, or, at the very least, excuse yourself by saying "*Shitsureishimasu*" ("Excuse me").

(b) Chewing gum while talking to someone. Never do this when on business or when meeting someone for the first time.
Putting the feet up on chairs or tables, touching someone with your foot, or sliding open a door with the foot.

(c) Kissing in public.

(d) Eating while walking in the street.

(e) Standing too close to someone while talking. The Japanese bow to each other in greeting rather than hugging, kissing or touching, and they stand quite far apart when talking.

INDEX

* Both English and Japanese terms, with the Japanese characters for the latter, are listed in the index below.

U

W

Y

Z

For Your TraveLife

英文 **日本絵とき事典2**

ILLUSTRATED

LIVING JAPANESE STYLE

初版 発行 　1984年11月20日
改訂15版 　1997年1月1日
　　　　　　（Jan. 1, 1997 15th edition）
編　集　人 　黒澤明夫
発　行　人 　岩田光正
発　行　所 　JTB 日本交通公社出版事業局
　　　　　　〒150 東京都渋谷区道玄坂1-10-8 渋谷野村ビル7階
印　刷　所 　交通印刷

●スタッフ
企画・編集 　JTB出版事業局　編集二部
　　　　　　外語図書編集　担当編集長　谷羽美紀
　　　　　　編集部直通　☎03-3477-9566
取材・編集協力 　アーバン・トランスレーション
イラスト 　松下正己
表紙デザイン 　東　芳純
翻　　訳 　John Howard Loftus

●JTB発行図書のご注文は
JTB出版販売センター
〒150 東京都渋谷区道玄坂1-10-8 渋谷野村ビル7階　☎03-3477-9588
●広告のお問合せは
JTB出版事業局広告部　☎03-3477-9531

964306　712032
ISBN4-533-01350-3